Cyberfutures

Cyberfutures

Culture and Politics on the
Information Superhighway

Edited by
Ziauddin Sardar
and Jerome R. Ravetz

Pluto  Press

First published 1996 by Pluto Press
345 Archway Road, London N6 5AA

Acknowledgements. Chapters 1, 2, 3 and 4 first appeared in *Futures*,
vol. 27, no. 7 (1995) and appear here in a modified form. The editors
are grateful to the publishers, Elsevier Science, for permission to use
them. Chapter 6 first appeared in *Current Anthropology*, vol. 35, no. 3
(1994). The editors are grateful to the publishers, University of
Chicago Press, for permission to use it in this volume.

British Library Cataloguing in Publication Data
A catalogue record for this book is available from the British Library

ISBN 0 7453 1120 2 hbk

Printing history: 02 01 00 99 98 97 96
10 9 8 7 6 5 4 3 2 1

Designed and produced for Pluto Press by
Chase Production Services, Chipping Norton, OX7 5QR
Typeset from disk by Stanford DTP Services, Milton Keynes
Printed in the EC by TJ Press, Padstow

Contents

List of Acronyms

A&E	Arts & Entertainment cable TV channel
AOL	America OnLine
ASCAP	American Society of Composers, Artists and Performers
AT&T	American Telephone and Telegraph
BBS	Bulletin Board System
CEO	Chief Executive Officer
FCC	Federal Communications Commission
FTP	File Transfer Protocol
HDTV	High-Definition Television
IRC	Internet Relay Chat (method for using the Internet to engage in real-time chats with others online)
ISDN	Integrated Services Digital Network (high speed phone lines for faster telecommunications throughput)
MBA	Master of Business Administration
MUD	Multi-User Dungeon or dimension (computer generated interactive reality)
NFL	National Football League
NSA	National Security Agency
OSI	The initials for the Federal department tracking down Nazi war criminals
PGP	Pretty Good Privacy – the encryption software that has become publicly distributed over the Net, for use in maintaining private E-mail
PPP	Point to Point Protocol – with SLIP one of the main protocols for linking to the Internet by phone
SIGGRAPH	Computer artists organisation which has an annual conference
S&L	Savings & Loan (similar to a Building Society in the UK)
SLIP	Serial Line Internet Protocol – with PPP one of the main protocols for linking to the Internet by phone
TCI-Sprint	Aborted merger attempt between TCI (big cable TV company) and Sprint (big phone company)

Introduction: Reaping the Technological Whirlwind

Ziauddin Sardar and Jerome R. Ravetz

The computer industry grows at a dazzling and dizzy speed. Its technical power seems to be increasing exponentially at least, its commercial base is broadening at an astonishing rate, and its penetration of society and individual lives appears to be becoming almost total. Within a matter of a few years, we have moved from clumsy 8-bit computers to the Pentium machines with startling computing power. Yesterday's Pacman and Alien Invaders are today's highly sophisticated interactive CD-ROMs; indeed, soon we will have Interactive Everything. We recently witnessed the coming of age of the Internet – the network of all the computer networks of the whole world. Now the World Wide Web is all the rage. We are communicating, working, shopping, learning and entertaining ourselves with computers. Some of us are even discovering carnal pleasures and God through the simple expedient of connecting our computers with a modem to the wide universe of cyberspace – the ether that lies inside and occupies the in-betweens of all the computers. We are now getting a first taste of 'Cyberia' – the new civilisation emerging through our human–computer interface and mediation.

To get some idea of the impact of this new technology on our world and the way we live in it, we might imagine that the telephone, television and the private automobile had all developed simultaneously, and in a matter of months rather than decades. For this new technology only starts by transforming the way we communicate with each other, play, receive information and learn. Our ideas of human interactions, even of our relationships with our bodies (and indeed with those of others) are bound to be transformed. How we see and value ourselves as persons, in relation to others and to society through 'work', are also up for drastic change. Of course, people will still live and die, work and play, love and hate, win and lose, as they always have. But the patterns in which all this takes place, and its meaning and experience, are due to be changed. Anyone who has travelled far abroad knows the experience of seeing the eternal constants of humanity appearing in different garb, both physical and emotional. Up to now, we have taken our own culture for granted as relatively stable in its essentials; now we must be ready for a cultural and existential earthquake.

Part of looking at ourselves anew is an appreciation of the role of free enterprise in the genesis and growth of this new force. Now, to be sure, private corporations rule all in the development of the hardware and also the basic software. But it is not quite the pure competitive market in which so many fervently believe. For there are monopolisitic influences which maintain dominance for products which are certainly not the best conceivable, but which are so deeply embedded that they can beat off all rivals indefinitely. More interesting, perhaps, is the role of the Government in the creation and fostering of this all-powerful technology. It can be seen as having started during the Second World War, with the promotion of powerful calculators; and then continuing after the war, when most experts imagined that only a handful of such machines would suffice for all industrial and scientific needs. But the big 'mainframes' soon found themselves constantly stretched; and eventually the 'personal computers' emerged from corporate development labs, and also inventors' garages, to start their long climb to dominance.

The move from isolated calculating machines to a network of communicators could not have happened spontaneously; and it is hard to imagine how private capital could take the plunge into such an unknowable future. But the Government, or more specifically Defence, was there with a concern about the preservation of a communications network after a major disruption. Some philosopher in their midst sold the idea of a decentralised network, invulnerable to being 'knocked out'; and so 'the Net' was born. Even its subsequent move to the civilian sector was largely a state-subsidised event, since it was universities and research establishments that created the elements of the Net as we know it.

This new technology then had a period of incubation, removed from the commercial sector and even from the general public. To be on the Net, you needed a 'server'; and this had to be within an institution that undertook financial and administrative responsibility for its share of the upkeep. So for some considerable time, only academics and researchers enjoyed the privileges of the Net; and they shaped it, as a social instrument, around their own needs and lifestyles. They formed an élite community that bears a strong resemblance to the informal 'colleges' of researchers, where the competition and rivalry takes place against a background of non-hierarchical relationships, exchange of unpaid services, and mutual trust. It is interesting to speculate whether the Net would have grown, or even survived, if at the moment of its creation it had been thrown into the hard world of the market place, where 'survival of the fittest' rather than 'mutual aid' is the motif.

Already the Net, enlarged and diluted as it now is, has fought three big battles for its integrity. The first was the easiest: the defence of 'Netiquette' against uncouth intruders. The earliest private servers bought into the Net, and their untutored subscribers mixed into its activities. They were quickly taught that although strong views and strong language are by no means excluded, there are rules about where and how they are to be used. A more serious incursion came from a commercial organisation that tried to use the Net for mass distribution of its advertisements. Here the reaction was more severe, where personal abuse was supplemented by sabotage of the firm's communications (telephone and fax) along with their E-mail capabilities. This might be called vigilante justice; but in the absence of a legal code (which would have its own enormous costs), such a prompt and universal reaction could be justifiable for the protection of the Net's integrity. If even one such attempt at mass advertising had been successful, then communications on the Net could have been quickly drowned in junk mail.

A more serious threat came from the Government, over the issue of secrecy. Here the technical issue is that it is all too easy for messages to be tapped or diverted by unauthorised persons interested in their contents. So security is to be protected by 'encryption', that is the coding of messages as they are sent. But this protection if far from absolute, either in principle or in practice. First, the Government's security agencies do not welcome the possibility of people sending messages that are absolutely impervious to scrutiny, even theirs. And second, every attempt at a secure code breeds people who want to break it, either for pleasure or for profit. Both these issues came to a head when the US Federal Government proposed its own coding system as a compulsory standard. They assured critics that such power would never be abused, in spite of some strong historical evidence to the contrary. And while the political debate was going on in a rather conventional fashion, the issue was decided on the Net. For various collections of people have shown, in various ways, that all the encryption methods so far offered as feasible, are capable of being broken, and without too much expenditure of new capital or labour time. The result is that encryption remains a matter for debate and decision, rather than a solution imposed by the institution with the most power.

The most recent battle has been on a more traditional ground, that of 'decency'. This was triggered by scare stories, in the US and abroad, that minors were being exposed to inappropriate materials, by the ease with which they could access locations on the Net that were nominally intended for adults only. Although libertarians dismissed all that as scaremongering, various administrative and technical systems for containing the problem were put into development. But the scare had reached the US Congress, and a bill which banned indecency on the Net slipped through the legislative process. It was scarcely noticed, and was opposed by very few; after all, who wants to face the electors as a friend of pornographers? But then a mighty roar was heard, as the existence of the legislation was realised, and its potential for abuse, mischief and confusion was appreciated. The Net's response included a symbolic black-out of many Web home pages (showing what censorship does), together with more traditional forms of organisation and protest. The standard American coalitions of pressure groups were enriched by a new ally: the judiciary, or at least some parts of it, who put the protest litigation into high gear, and secured some protection for those who might be at risk under the legislation.

Those three campaigns show how the Net has established an identity, not merely among its aficionados, but also on the national scene. How well it will maintain this, once is it has undergone the inevitable processes of diffusion attendant on growth, remains to be seen. But as a special interest lobby, comparable to all those others that enliven the American political scene, it is unique in being defined by the means to communicate and organise in the protection of its interests. Of course, not all those who venture into Cyberia are active citizens of the Net; and as participation grows, the veterans and activists may become a minority so small as to become unrepresentative and ultimately sectarian. On that, only time will tell.

For most users, activity is at an unsophisticated level, both technically and politically. The mushrooming Bulletin Boards serve many special interests, most laudable, but some (as militia and Fascists) not so. Some fear that the polity will fragment into closed groups who need no other communication than the reinforcement of their fantasies through the Net; others are sure that many citizens hitherto excluded from contacts will experience new connections and new empowerment. Both are probably right, to some extent; the open question is which tendency will become dominant, numerically and in political significance. As the hardware develops further, and the materials available on the Net (and through other media) become ever more vivid and sophisticated, then the cultural implications will be profound. How they will affect our lives, with what mixture of good and evil, and how all this might be controlled by or on behalf of the public, are issues which are discussed in the chapters of this volume.

Here the reader will find a critical stance, which up to now has not been common among commentaries on Cyberia. Of course, we are assured on all sides that this progress will have profound effects on work, culture, leisure – everything, including our humanity. Yet, just what these effects will be, how good and evil will be distributed among them, and what anyone will be able to do about things they do not like, are issues which are left on the sidelines. Aside from an occasional panic over 'cyber-porn' accessible to children, the picture is overwhelmingly one of an indistinct glow. Critical studies are labelled as by 'Neo-Techno-CRYPTO-CYBER-LUDDITES' by *Whole Earth*'s cyber-guru Howard Rheingold.[1] He calls for 'more critical thinking from those of us who embrace and endorse technology', as if there has already been more than enough from the others.

One possible reason for this dearth of effective critical commentary is that it is genuinely very difficult to make a sensible analysis, based on reliable information and offering reasonable prospects, with limited pleasures and controllable worries. This is why in this book we do not attempt predictions and judgements of the usual sort. Instead, we have tried to examine the underlying assumptions and values of the cyberspace revolution that is unfolding before our eyes. Our goal was not to furnish a balanced set of sensible surveys of various aspects of Cyberia, nor to provide a 'blueprint' for action or even suggestions of the sorts of institutions and attitudes that will be required if this new technology is to serve humanity and not derange us. We set out to question the absolute faith that is being exhibited in the goodness of cybertechnologies and their ability to enhance the quality of life.

For this we make no apologies. So deep is society's collective ignorance of what cybertechnologies are doing to us that the first urgent task is to discover our ignorance. That is accomplished here, indirectly, by these chapters which send searchlight beams into an obscure future. Then we can begin to make out some of the lines of development, at least on those aspects that are easier to forecast, such as employment and mass culture. Beyond that, we can only, for now, savour the various cultural currents and tsunamis that might be encountered in the coming decades. As reality becomes ever more artefactual and unstable, the inherited barriers to the rule of fantasy are weakened; and the future may turn out to be a weird rearrangement of the elements out of which we have constructed our lived world of 'ordinary' experience. And we can use our speculation on this weird future as a means of reflecting on ourselves and on the assumptions we have inherited about the way the world is, should be, and yet could be.

Ziauddin Sardar's chapter sets the tone for this collection, viewing Cyberia as a set of interacting fantasies, in this case those which are rooted in Europe's imperial past of political and cultural conquest. In his chapter, the focus is on the 'dark', or perhaps 'flip' side of Western civilisation, those aspects which official culture and analysis prefer not to recognise. Sardar explains that the West (starting in Renaissance Europe) has always been obsessed with new territories to conquer. Cyberspace is the surrogate for old colonies, the 'new continent' artificially created to satisfy Western man's insatiable desire to acquire new wealth and riches. He draws strong parallels between the subjugation of non-Western cultures and the colonisation of cyberspace: the use of the colonial metaphors, not least that of 'the frontier'; the common quest for new markets; the similarities between the practices of the old Imperial syndicates like the English and Dutch East India Companies and the new hardware and software corporations, the obsession in both cases with violence and sex; the rampage of adventurers and perverts; and the projections of the darker side of the West on newly conquered territories. Sardar's thesis is that cyberspace is the newly discovered Other of Western civilisation, and it will be subjected to the same treatment that the West handed out to all non-Western cultures. But this time there is an ironic twist: the darker side of the West, projected on cyberspace, immediately bounces right back on the West itself – with all its all too evident consequences.

Returning to the civilisation that is giving birth to Cyberia, there is one thing of which we can be reasonably sure: we are in the early stages of a revolution. But, what sort of revolution it is, where it is taking us, and what we can do about it, individually and collectively, is yet completely obscure. The new revolution, which both Jerry Ravetz and George Spencer describe as 'microcybernetic' to emphasise both its 'micro' nature and total emphasis on 'control' ('cybernetics' is after the Greek word for 'steering' or 'control'), is quite unprecedented in our recent history. For the past half-millennium, deep changes in our social and intellectual structures have been the subject of analysis and debate even as they got under way. Not merely those deriving from a clear overall conception, like the Renaissance and the Scientific Revolution, but even those which were just happening, like the Industrial Revolution, gave rise to critical reflections which became classics in their own right and helped to shape the common understanding of the process and thereby the process itself. But now we are in what might be the biggest revolution of them all, and so far the experts seem to have very little to say beyond detail and platitudes. And the media, as the computer and online pages of quality newspapers typify, are happy simply wallowing in the gee-whiz excitement of new developments – with an occasional foray into scaremongering on the obvious issues. If we say that this is not because of the lack of intelligence or concern, then we are learning something very important about this process which is now engulfing the worlds of industry, commerce, culture and lived experience.

What differentiates the cyber-revolution from previous revolutions is that it is a revolution in consciousness. As Jerry Ravetz argues, we are in a transitional generation with cyberspace: the admiration of 'faster than thought' machines has been well tamed, and we now move to the manipulation of structures and images and the creation of patterns of sensations. The novelty of the new technology is that it operates so much at deep levels of consciousness. Physical and material worlds have apparently been conquered and rendered fluid by technology; now it is the turn of cognition. Cybertechnology is a runaway state as well as being the *raison d'être* of state. The future will be shaped by two kinds of generations, one experiencing ever more intoxicating powers, while the other a deeper and deeper hopelessness. Worse: the momentum of cybertechnology does not allow time for reflection, viable dissent or a change of direction. 'The disturbing prospect', Ravetz writes, 'is that opposition to the microcybernetic consumerist dictatorship will find its only effective location deep underground, in the hands of zealots or fanatics who are content to destroy without bothering to dialogue. And microcybernetic technology is particularly vulnerable to just such a sort of opposition.'

Ravetz's thoughts are complemented by George Spencer, who describes microcybernetics as a meta-technology. It is unique in history, different from all previous technologies, in that 'it empowers the most general possible technology, that which enters into the control of all processes, all other technologies, and itself. In doing so, it displaces or transforms all other means of control, notably those involving human limbs and minds.' It operates only at the level of control, and its power is independent of content. Thus, the very nature of this technology means that there are no recognisable limits to its penetration and displacement of 'labour'; it is a fulfilment of the capitalist dream of 'more for less'. We are thus faced with a future where not only human labour is totally redundant but also where we cannot even contemplate discovery or design of new specifications for control that only humans can fulfil. But as this process bites ever deeper into the productive process, we will have increasing numbers who are not merely deprived of the power to purchase and consume, but who are, in this society where work makes us real, stripped of dignity and meaning in their lives. In this way, the enhancement of production by microcybernetics becomes deeply subversive of the whole socio-technical order in which it takes place.

Similarly, the radical movement needs to be aware of cyberspace as the new will to power. Vivian Sobchack starts her chapter at a point that seems remote from Cyberia: the two notions of 'franchise'

that have coexisted in the United States: one connoting freedom,
as voting; and the other connoting property and privilege, as a
McDonald's or the Los Angeles Rams football team. But these come
together in the working out of the contradictions in the propaganda
for Cyberia; for its transformations of experience seem to offer new
freedoms, but do so only within existing commercial and cultural
constraints. Hence, as in the Bay Area publication *Mondo 2000*,
political messages become totally confused, and cynicism finally
becomes Utopian. For those still interested in reality, her message
is that Cyberia will be profoundly dialectical: enhancing and
reducing, freeing and enslaving, unifying and dividing, all along
new lines that emerge out of old structures, but never transgressing
the boundaries of power.

The dialectical character of Cyberia is further developed by
Nigel Clark. He shows how, in spite of the apparent separateness,
and mutual hostility, of the cultures of information and of 'ecology',
they interpenetrate in surprising and significant ways. It is not
merely the case that 'nature' is, in our apprehension, always
mediated by technique; thus the environmental enthusiasts of the
1960s onwards had at least partly derived their vision from Disney's
cartoon films of cuddly fawns. Also, both Ecology and Cyberia
started as countercultural movements, with a point of contact in
the *Whole Earth Catalog*. Now we find that the prophets on both
sides convey a vision of some pure and unmediated reality, 'out
there' either on a landscape where the observer is absent in spite
of his presence, or where the technology of illusion has become
totally transparent and the fantasy is unadulterated. The dialectical
unity of the two spheres fits well with the insights of postmodernism;
thus while some have said that virtual reality is a simulation whose
function is to make the real world seem more real, it is equally true
that pristine nature is a simulation which serves to make the other
realities less real. With the commodification of leisure, of 'natural'
values, and their management through increasingly high technology
devices, all distinctions of the two realms will become increasingly
blurred. This might serve as a corrective to their separate fantasies,
or perhaps as food for a syncretic super-fantasy of the whole human
experience.

In the same vein, Arturo Escobar suggest that the same tools
that the West used to study and enframe the Other with, should
now be applied to cyberculture. Escobar puts cybertechnologies
in their broader context in terms of what is happening in complexity,
chaos theory and biotechnologies and asks in what ways the relations
between First and Third World are restructured in the light of new
technologies. What, in fact, is the political economy of cyberculture?
Given that cybertechnology, particularly virtual reality, is likely to
continue to be circumscribed by military and economic interests,

and that despite its much touted potential for liberatory and humanising purposes, the military and profit-orientated applications will undoubtedly remain dominant, how will various groups of people negotiate specific forms of power, authority, representation and knowledge? What new forms of social construction of reality, and of negotiation of such construction, are being created or modified? How are people socialised by their routine experience of constructed spaces created by new technologies? Would it be possible to produce ethnographic accounts of the multiplicity of practices linked to the new technologies in various social, regional and ethnic settings? How do these practices relate to broader social issues, such as the control of labour, the accumulation of capital, the organisation of life-worlds, and the globalisation of cultural production? Escobar, raising a stream of questions just waiting to be investigated, considers that anthropology can re-enter the real world by tackling the new 'story of life' as it is being lived today and as it is shaping the future.

Finally, Jay Kinney uses current American experience as evidence for his exploration of the political and social contradictions of Cybersociety. He contrasts two current scenarios, libertarian Utopia and corporatist Dystopia; one is based on vision and hype and the other on continuing relations of power and control. It is as likely as anything else, that the scenarios will both develop and mix, leading to severe confusion in the short run and ultimately the dissolution of our inherited social, institutional and cultural structures. As an example, 'Perhaps the World Wide Web will be like really good crack: cheap and affordable until you're thoroughly addicted, then you wake up one day to discover the meter ticking and you've got an insatiable hunger for online informercials.' And in spite of the prevalence of online democracy, 'I have a recurring dream where the new political paradigm is already in place: you have to wear Nikes and I have to wear Reeboks – it's in the fine print of our software licences.'

This array of perspectives may seem inconclusive, perhaps even bewildering. But that is no mistake; the phenomena of this ongoing revolution are, on analysis, bewildering to those who have grown up in an age when information was unproblematic and consciousness not for sale. But the new reality, as this culturally explosive technology impacts on a cultural system already in crisis, defies simple analysis and management. The total and enthusiastic embrace of cybertechnologies in the fantasy of finding 'new markets' for economic growth, and misplaced aspirations of finding nirvana, along with the 'moral panic' they have produced, is a product of our postmodern times. Extreme reactions come naturally in a society where nothing is permanent, institutions of traditional authority stand discredited, and no one is immune from anything.

Cyberculture simultaneously fragments and isolates as well as organises and controls. Unpredictably subversive, it corrodes the boundary between the official and the 'flip' side of culture, so that decorum, the necessary constraint for behaviour that is civilised, becomes an antiquated, forgotten category.

Were we to try to express all this confusion in a single phrase, it would be the working out of 'the fantasy of fantasies'. For in cyberspace we have a kaleidoscopic jumbling together of partial and fragmented visions of reality, where each one is hegemonic in its own domain. Overriding them all is the fantasy that drives the fantasy industry, now the great engine of 'growth', where the creation of consumer demands is the key sector that provides such 'jobs' and hence such real pay packets that survive. It was the countercultural prophet Ted Roszak who, in *The Cult of Information*,[2] first called attention to the similarities between faith in relics of the True Cross and faith in computers as emblems of salvation. The apparently simple credulities of the Medieval 'Age of Faith' are now so far behind us that they are nearly forgotten; yet the proud Enlightenment belief that science renders us immune from such fantasies, has become the foundation of another sort of delusion.

The main roots of this new fantasy of fantasies lie (as Vivian Sobchack indicates) in the contemporary industry of illusion, of which 'Hollywood' is the symbol. It is a long time gone since preachers could stoke up the imagination of their flocks with visions of the delights of Heaven and the terrors of Hell, and thereby help to maintain personal prudence and social stability. The gap left by the secularisation of culture has been filled, and now overfilled, by the commercialised, synthetic fantasies on the various screens, large and small, public and, increasingly, private. The viewing public is always encouraged to create its own confusion between its lived reality and its perceived hyper-reality, as in the stream of titillation about the private lives of the 'stars'; and now that the manufactured reality becomes ever more intense and intimate, the distinction becomes more blurred.

So far that is simple fantasy; the fantasy of fantasies arises among those who create and promote this new sophistic, meretricious reality. For their survival depends less and less on solid knowledge and past achievements, and ever more on lucky guesses about the confluences of technologies, fashions and finance at a point in time just beyond the planning horizon. So the whole industry, and all the cultural worlds around it, are deprived of the sorts of reality-testing once provided, however coarsely, by the box office and the casting couch. The condition of fantasy of fantasies is well exhibited in *Wired*, the most detached and reflective of the mass circulation journals servicing the industry and its culture. There, amid the adverts for yet newer astounding gadgets, is portrayed, in rich and vivid detail, a universe of fantasy about fantasy. It is all about 'images' and their makers; what is happening now, what might be happening soon; and all totally self-contained. The outside world intrudes only when there is some threat to the normal operations of the system, as in censorship or snooping by the Government. The problems of natural and social worlds becoming increasingly stressed by the same sorts of developments which produce the Infobahn, are, it seems, totally irrelevant to the glossy fantasies of the Net-visions. Now, any trade journal necessarily focuses on the reality which concerns its members; there is no special dereliction in that. But since this is now becoming the technology of technologies, which is intended to transform production, society and consciousness all together, the hothouse creatures of *Wired* will, for its readers and those they influence, tend to become surrogates for anything that might have grown on its own outside.

There are two sorts of problems with fantasies: while they last, they suck many people into worlds of delusion; and when they collapse, they leave a lot of wreckage, human and social, behind. Societies not ruled by science have the historic experience of regularly recurring fantasies, usually religious in content, about impending visitations that will make everyone happy and good. In modern, secular societies, fantasies have usually been restricted to dedicated reformers who have believed that their sector, be it education, government, science or production, held the key to redemption. Their private visions would animate public campaigns which would then embark on their own careers in an uncomprehending and uncaring world. A primarily hedonistic mass fantasy had to wait for the counterculture of the 1960s; and now Cyberia is, in its operations, nearly totally narcissistic.

Historians have studied what happens when fantasies collapse; when the leader recants to save his head, or the cargo does not arrive, or worldly success brings worldly corruption. Normally, mechanisms of denial and reinterpretation enable some to keep their faith; but others just drift away. In the case of entire social systems when the fantasy loses credibility, years of disorganisation and distress may be endured until a new order emerges. With the fantasy element of cyberspace, the collapse would start as with any addictive drug; the euphoria requires ever larger hits for its production, and causes ever deeper depressions in its absence. For we live in our bodies, which need to be kept fed, warm and clean by flows of real materials and energy; and we need comradeship and love from other real people. No virtual reality can substitute these primary needs; and a society which discarded them in the pursuit of electronic happiness would soon become so dysfunctional that the system itself could easily become subject to corruption and sabotage from within.

When, as now, we are dealing with a fantasy of fantasies, in which not merely the mass experience but also the means of its production become a part of a factitious social and subjective reality, the prospects of a collapse become awesome. The rather stately progression to disaster described in E.M. Forster's *The Machine Stopped*[3] would not happen here. Rather, one could imagine recurring crises of confidence in the prospect of unending exponential growth, quality being lost in all aspects of the system, administrative and financial systems degrading towards chaos, kids stumbling around blindly as their VR (virtual reality) goggles go blank, and people trying desperately to put some meaning into the cataclysm which leaves them defenceless against the raw forces of envy and hate which, by their experiential privileges, they had all unwittingly provoked. Equally, one could imagine the creativity unleashed by the new media enabling the system to hold itself together technically, until it transforms itself into something qualitatively different and better. Who knows?

The prospect of the extinction of civilisation as we know it has been with us for some decades, first with nuclear war and now with environmental change. Hence it should not be shocking to consider all the fantasies and their associated contradictions in the context of yet another challenge to our civilisation. Certainly, the cyberfuture is only an accentuation of the dynamic, aggressive, unstable style of European civilisation, which has been obvious for the last half-millennium, and perhaps longer. The microcybernetic technologies of the present and near future, soon to interact with microbiological technology for the transformation of production and perhaps of life as well, can be seen as just another successor to those innovators who broke asunder the fetters of production of the Medieval guilds, and also to those European predators who were let loose on the civilisations of other continents.

We can imagine European civilisation as a vast experiment in social organisation and human consciousness; where the bounds on individualised self-awareness and mass material consumption have been shattered, and 'progress' has become an unquestioned good. Forever revolutionising itself, Europe has arrived at a point where the next revolution might be the deepest imaginable. We already know that nuclear weaponry can truly make a world war impossible for a long time to come, simply by destroying its basis in material culture; and we know that the natural environment cannot continue to be a sink for the unsolved problems of our material and social existence. Now we are facing a new revolution that will combine a multitude of the paradoxical and contradictory trends of our civilisation as it has developed so far. It will liberate in some ways, and enslave in others; it will enlarge consciousness in some ways, and destroy self-respect in others; it will enable greater human compassion in some ways, and also unleash the ugly Other within ourselves; and through its subversive enhancement of control for particular tasks, it will create an engine of innovation that defies societal control. Europe has been defined up to now (particularly from the outside) by conquest; and now we face the prospect of conquest, not even by external super-intelligent beings, but from the inside by a plague of robots of our own making.

What will emerge for civilisation as this technological whirlwind yields its harvest, is at the moment totally impossible to predict. And this is perhaps the greatest lesson of cyberfutures. Our technology is now truly out of control; our ignorance of its consequences completely swamps our knowledge. This crucial impotence and ignorance, combined with the intoxicating mass fantasy of Cyberia, make this revolution unique among all those that humankind has hitherto experienced. Since we cannot know, predict or control it, our only path now is to comprehend the novelty and depth of the process, and thereby to be more aware of what man, not God, has wrought.

Notes

1. Howard Rheingold, 'Neo-Techno-CRYPTO-CYBER-LUDDITIES', *Whole Earth Review*, Winter 1995, pp. 100–103.
2. Theodore Roszak, *The Cult of Information*, (Cambridge, Lutterworth, 1986).
3. E.M. Forster, 'The Machine Stopped', in *Collected Short Stories*, (Harmondsworth, Penguin Books, 1954).

CHAPTER 1

alt.civilizations.faq
Cyberspace as the Darker Side of the West

Ziauddin Sardar

Richard Pepin's *Hologram Man* is a third grade film with a first class insight into Western psychosis. It exhibits and plays with all that Western man desires, all that lies buried deep in his consciousness and all that is steaming his restless soul. The story is quite one-dimensional. A rookie cop, Decoda, arrests a psychotic terrorist, Slash Gallagher, after a bloody encounter. In his own evil way, Slash just wants the world to be a better place and free of the Corporation that rules it; and in his own legal way, Decoda too just wants the world to be a better place and doesn't really care for the Corporation that sustains him. Slash is sentenced to the worst form of imprisonment that the future can offer: holographic stasis. His body is turned into a hologram, while his brain and soul are stored in a computer to be reprogrammed. Slash's multicultural gang (this is a policially correct film) manage to free their leader, hacking his mind and soul out of the computer, but his body is destroyed in the attempt. Slash pours an artificial skin on himself and walks the earth as an electromagnetic hologram: walking through walls, changing his physical identity at will, a mind, a soul, free from the limitations of physical existence he is invincible, a man turned into god by virtual reality. As is usual with such narratives, Decoda too turns into a hologram to defeat and capture his foe. Even though he is not as strong as Slash, Decoda is smarter. In the final encounter, Decoda not only kills Slash but also takes care of the equally evil chairman of the Corporation.

The tone of *Hologram Man* is set within the first ten minutes of the film: grand spectacle wrapped in grotesque violence and graphic sex. Its origins in computer games like 'Doom 2' and 'Mortal Kombat' are evident, as is its love affair with digital technology, which played no small part in its production, and virtual reality. Such combinations of violence, advanced technology and sex are not only used to sell films and video games (they are the *raison d'être* of *Hologram Man* and numerous other similar films like *Digital Man*, *Brain Scan*, *Videodrome* and *Lawnmower Man*), they also come in rather useful in shaping civilisations. Violence, advanced technology and sex have been the containers – vats – within which the West has existed for much of the second half of the millennium. In the normal course of events, the West has used these barrels to capture non-Western civilisations and cultures and then projected its own darker side on to them, portraying and describing – and therefore containing – them in terms of violence, sex and primitive technology. At the end of the second millennium, however, the standard grand narrative appears to be going through a new and interesting twist: the darker side of the West is bouncing back on itself. The very materials with which the West painted all Other civilisations is now acquiring a life of its own and is threatening to recast the projected image as well as the self-perception of the West. As the body of Western civilisation gradually dissolves into digital technology, it is slowly being replaced, just like those of Slash and Decoda in *Hologram Man*, with a transparent virtual skin that reveals the true darkness that lies underneath: in the mind and soul of the West. Decoda and Slash are the two Janus-like faces of Western civilisation: one, the projected innocence, standard-bearer of civilisation, the enforcer of universal law and morals; the other, pathologically untamed, the psychotic inner reality. To look at the inner reality of the West, the darker side it projects on to Other cultural and mental landscapes, we must look at the West's latest conquest, the new domain that it has colonised: cyberspace.

The Allure of the Colon

Western civilisation has always been obsessed with new territories to conquer. The narratives of these conquests, on the whole, have followed a basic, linear pattern. The hunger for new conquests stems from the insatiable desire to acquire new wealth and riches which in turn provides impetus for the development of new technologies of subjugation which are then employed to bring new territories under the servitude of the West. Once a new territory has been colonised, it is handed over to business interests to loot; and the worst elements of the West are posted there to administer and civilise the natives. The natives themselves are rendered non-people by framing them with the images of all that the West fears about itself. Cristobal Colon's (aka Columbus) voyage to the 'New World', for example, was a product of the quest for wealth and riches, what in contemporary parlance we would call 'new markets'. Colon and those who followed him, adventurers and perverts, rampaged what they discovered and butchered the natives they encountered. The West's conquest and colonisation of the Muslim world was motivated by its image of the Orient where unfathomable riches existed and cruel and barbaric scenes were staged. Once colonised,

Islam was projected as evil and depraved, licentious and barbaric, ignorant and stupid, monstrous and ugly, fanatic and violent: the very traits of those who went to the Muslim world to rule it, civilise it, and strip it of its wealth and power. The English and Dutch East India Companies went to India and Indonesia looking for new markets and, with the aid of advanced military technology, enslaved their cultures and turned these countries into gold mines for the homeland. The conquest of the American West was spurred by the Gold Rush, the desire of the settlers for absolute freedom, and ended with the almost total annihilation of the native Americans. When the West ran out of physical landscapes to conquer, it moved into mental territories. Colonisation paved the way for modernity. During the second half of this century, modernity relentlessly conquered almost every culture and every mind. Under colonisation, the basic weapon was the brute force of military technology; modernity combines military technology with communication technology, Western cultural products and instrumental rationality. The 'civilising mission' gives way to 'progress' and 'modernisation' and produces the same effect: cultures are decimated, bulldozed, 'globalised' with barbaric abandon. When mental and cultural territories are exhausted, the West moves on to conquer the reality of Other people. The end of modernity ushers in the all-embracing totality of postmodernism. In Other peoples' reality, Other ways of knowing and being, Other identities, postmodernism has discovered new spaces to conquer and subdue. Here 'progress', 'modernisation' and instrumental rationality are replaced with relativism, real human beings are filtered through electronic screens to render them into virtual images – all the better to exploit them and butcher them without feeling real emotions.[1] Virtual persons bleed virtual blood – just like so many computer games, including that simulation of the real thing, 'War in the Gulf'.[2]

Beyond postmodernism's subjugation of the realities, modes of knowing and actual being of Other cultures, the West urgently needs new spaces to conquer. The moon and the inner planets are ruled out for the time being given the cost of colonising them. The outer space is a domain best left, for the time being, to *Star Trek*. For the conquest to continue unabated, new terrestrial territories have to be found; and where they don't actually exist, they must be created. Enter, cyberspace.

Like most new technologies, cyberspace did not appear, to use the words of Chris Chesher, 'from nowhere as a mystical spark of inspiration from the mind of one individual'.[3] It is a conscious reflection of the deepest desires, aspirations, experiential yearning and spiritual *Angst* of Western man. It is resolutely being designed as a new market and it is an emphatic product of the culture, world-view and technology of Western civilisation. That it is a 'new frontier', a 'new continent', being reclaimed from some unknown wilderness by heroic figures not unlike Cristobal Colon, is quite evident from how the conquest of cyberspace is described by many of its champions. Analogies to colonisation abound. The September 1990 edition of the cyberpunk magazine, *Mondo 2000*, carries the cover line: 'The Rush Is On! Colonizing Cyberspace'.[4] Ivan Pope, editor of the British cyberspace magazine *3W*, describes it as 'one of those mythical places, like the American West or the African Interior, that excites the passions of explorers and carpetbaggers in equal measures'.[5] Howard Rheingold, a guru of the movement, describes his own flirtations with cyberspace as 'my own odyssey to the outposts of a new scientific frontier ... and an advanced glimpse of a possible new world in which reality itself might become a manufactured and metered commodity'.[6] Many computer games, like 'Super Mario Brothers', 'Civilization', 'Death Gate', 'Merchant Colony' and 'Big Red Adventure' are little more than updated versions of the great European voyages of discovery. These are not just games but worlds, constructed Western Utopias, where all history can be revised and rewritten, all non-Western people forgotten, in the whirl of the spectacle. It is hardly surprising that Mary Fuller and Henry Jenkins have found direct parallels between many Nintendo games and New World documents like Columbus's *Diario* (1492–93), Walter Raleigh's *Discoveries of the large, rich and beautiful empire of Guiana* (1596) and John Smith's *True Relation of such occurrences and accidents of noate as hath hapned in Virginia* (1608). The theme is reflected in more serious documents. 'Cyberspace and the American Dream: A Magna Carta for the Knowledge Age', a document that 'represents the cumulative wisdom and innovation of many dozens of people' including Alvin Toffler, prepared for the right-wing The Progress and Freedom Foundation, states that 'the bioelectronic frontier is an appropriate metaphor for what is happening in cyberspace, calling in mind as it does the spirit of invention and discovery that led the ancient mariners to explore the world, generations of pioneers to tame the American continent and, more recently, to man's first exploration of outer space'.[7] We are not told what the voyages of discovery did to the indigenous populations; nor that they were motivated as much by greed as the so-called 'spirit of adventure'.[8] Unlike the original Magna Carta, which concerned itself with mundane political and civil liberties granted by King John at Runnymede on 15 June 1215, 'A Magna Carta for the Knowledge Age' places cyberspace at the zenith of civilisation: it represents 'civilization's truest, highest calling' and would lead to unparalleled 'demassification, customization, individuality, freedom', providing the main form of 'glue holding together an increasingly free and diverse society'.

Cyberspace, then, is the 'American dream' writ large; it marks the dawn of a new 'American civilisation'. White man's burden shifts from its moral obligation to civilise, democratise, urbanise and colonise non-Western cultures, to the colonisation of cyberspace. Those engaged in constructing the new cybercivilisation often see their heroic efforts in terms of 'a moral responsibility to fulfil an historic destiny, comparing themselves with historical precedents, like the original White colonizers of North America'.[9]

The 'frontier' was, of course, an invented concept which recapitulated an experience that had already passed. The frontier exists in the mind, it operates as a myth only after the process of control has been established. The fate of the American West was already determined before the idea of the frontier could be effective as the means for its dominated integration within the praxis of American citizenry.[10] As an idea, the frontier is a tool of domination that arises from the certainty that one already has total control. As an instrument, the function of the frontier is to pass the routine practice of domination into the hands of the populace, to give them the illusion of freedom while they merely act out the actual effective control that is already predetermined, scrutinised and seen to be good by those with power. The frontier is the agency through which power élites get everyone to do their work while thinking they are acting on their own volition. Cyberspace frontier is no different. It has already been controlled; the populace are now being motivated to explore and settle in the new frontier. The ideologically constructed anarchy of cyberspace reflects the drive of the early settlers who colonised the territory like free agents, but only as the free agents of the evolving concept of a particular civilisation. What the frontier gives is the liberty to indulge licence within the brief of the civilisational stage directions, 'to do', as John Wayne apocryphally termed it, 'what a man's got to do'. What such men did turned out to be only what was in the self-interest of the civilisation they represented, and what characterised the doing was brutality to Others.

What the cyberspace 'frontier' is doing as a first step is rewriting history: an exercise in catharsis to release the guilt of wiping out numerous indigenous cultures from the face of the earth, the colonisation of two-thirds of the world and the continuous degradation of life in the Third World that the West has engendered. Why else have these colonial metaphors of discovery been adopted by champions of cyberspace – particularly, as Mary Fuller and Henry Jenkins note, when these

> metaphors are undergoing sustained critique in other areas of the culture, a critique that hardly anyone can be unaware of in the year after the quincentenary of Columbus's first American

landfall. When John Barlow (1990) writes that 'Columbus was probably the last person to behold so much usable and unclaimed real estate (or unreal estate) as these cybernauts have discovered' (p. 37), the comparison to cyberspace drains out the materiality of the place Columbus discovered, and the nonvirtual bodies of the pre-Columbian inhabitants who did, in fact, claim it, however unsuccessfully. I would speculate that part of the drive behind the rhetoric of virtual reality as a New World or new frontier is the desire to recreate the Renaissance encounter with America without guilt: this time, if there are others present, they really won't be human (in the case of Nintendo characters), or if they are, they will be other players like ourselves, whose bodies are not jeopardized by the virtual weapons we wield.[11]

But, of course, cyberspace does have real victims. The rewriting of colonial history has a direct impact on the lives of those whose history is being denied and whose historic identity is distorted. It leads to blaming the victims for the misery of their current reality. If Colon, Drake and other swashbuckling heroes of Western civilisation were no worse than pioneers of cyberspace, then they must have been a good thing; and colonised people should be thankful for the civilisation and new technology they brought and the new markets they opened up! Western revisionist writers and thinkers never tire of making such claims, as William A Henry III's reinterpretation of American history in his *In Defense of Elitism* illustrates so well.[12] Cyberspace is particularly geared towards the erasure of all non-Western histories. Once a culture has been 'stored' and 'preserved' in digital forms, opened up to anybody who wants to explore it from the comfort of their armchair, then it becomes more real than the real thing. Who needs the arcane and esoteric real thing anyway? In the postmodern world where things have systematically become monuments, nature has been transformed into 'reserve', knowledge is giving way to information and data, it is only a matter of time before Other people and their cultures become 'models', so many zeros and ones in cyberspace, exotic examples for scholars, voyeurs and other interested parties to load on their machine and look at. Cyberspace is a giant step forward towards museumisation of the world: where anything remotely different from Western culture will exist only in digital form. And in digital form, not only their past but also their present and potential futures can be manipulated: 'We can run a simulation and show you what are your best options for survival.' But non Western history is being sanitised not just by the metaphors cyberspace, numerous computer and video games, advertiser for software, but also by a host of new CD-ROM encycl like *Microsoft Encarta*, the *Compton Interactive Encyclope*

Star Trek's Captain Pecard is your tour guide, and *The Story of Civilization* by Will and Ariel Durant. The great explosion of information on CD-ROMS is an old West-is-Great paradigm repackaged for a new generation and extending the dominance of the old academy. The hard won new spaces and discourses of Third World perspectives created in conventional fields now disappear into the oblivion of cyberspace: we thus return to square one, the beginning. The Other is once again the virgin land waiting passively to be dominated by the latest territory controlled by the West. Even the documentary evidences of history are oxidised in the way they are 'preserved' in cyberspace:

> The Archivo General de Indias in Seville harbours hundreds of thousands of historical sources, in the form of decrees, instructions, letters, regulations, case records, maps, petitions from Indian chiefs, etc. which refer to the historical ties between Spain and its former colonies in Latin America. The whole archive is now being digitalised. The manuscripts are being recorded on interactive, optical video disc, not only to protect the original collection [*to preserve the past for posterity – the present is once again discarded*], but also to increase their accessibility for the researcher: the documents, discoloured by time, can be 'cleaned' on the screen via the computer (stains can be removed, creased smoothed out, colours changed, letters enlarged or reduced, etc ...). In a way, a 'contaminated' and guilt-laden episode of history is being relieved of its blood, sweat and tears, and being given a false air of innocence. In the unbearable lightness of the realm of data, things are being relieved of their stoutness and weightiness: as 'bits' and 'bytes' they all look the same. It is not about whether the originals speak the truth, but about their disappearance into a retouchable 'image': the act of copying makes the originals artificial, too. At the same time, the 'real thing', having become inaccessible, is entrenched in secrecy for fear that it will be touched by life, so that its existence becomes insignificant.[13]

But cyberspace not only kills history, it kills people too. The dress rehearsal for the smart bombs that so consistently missed their ~~in the~~ Gulf War was carried out in cyberspace. Cyberspace, ~~~~ hi-fi and so much of modern advanced ~~~~ rigins in the military. The Internet was ~~~~ oof mode of communication in case of a ~~~~ anded as a computer network that linked ~~~~ ntres with the defence departments. Virtual ~~~~ rged as a safe and inexpensive way of training ~~~~ military planes. Indeed, the US military has ~~~~ nt and operators using VR technology for some time. The origins of the term 'information superhighway' can be traced back to that other highway, also a product of military concerns, which emerged at the end of the Second World War: the grand American interstate highway system (the Al Gores have been involved in both: Al Gore Sr played an instrumental part in the development of the federal highway system; Al Gore Jr has been instrumental in placing the information superhighway on the American political agenda). The software games market is saturated with 'shoot-em-up' games and flight simulators, involving flying jet fighters, shooting and bombing targets, not simply because people like playing such games, but because weapons guidance and tracking research for military use has filtered down into video games. Virtual reality has now moved on to the 'entertainment' arena largely because the US defence industry wants a return on its investment by finding other uses for the technology it originally developed.[14]

Not surprisingly, the first major commercial application of VR betrays its military origins. Battle Tech, one of the earliest commercial uses of VR, is a game based on networked military tank simulators. At Chicago's North Pier, where a Battle Tech Center opened in 1990,

> Players pay and sign in at the front desk and are matched up with others to make teams. The teams play in a room decorated as the war room of a starship, with TV monitors filling up a wall. Each player gets a Battle Tech console, which is steered like a battle tank, with floor pedals and throttle. Speakers around the players supply the sounds of machinery and battle. The joystick has triggers and buttons for controlling weapons systems. The idea is not to beat the machine but to beat the enemy either individually or in teams. As one report states, 'what gives realism and challenge to the Battle Tech experience is the fact that you play against living opponents rather than the algorithms of a computer's program'.[15]

Once the military has opened up the new frontier, the settlers can move in to play their games, to explore, colonise and exploit the new territory taking us back to mythic times when there were other worlds (Islam, China, India, Africa, America) with resources beyond imagination and riches without limits.

Since its genesis as a military research project, the Internet has been managed by the government-funded National Science Foundation (NSF). The NSF has now handed over the managerial reins to three commercial carriers, Sprint, Ameritech and Pacific Bell. These multinational, modern equivalents of the East India Company will become the principal providers of access to the Internet. The many networks that make the Internet, the network of all computer networks, are interlinked in a rough hierarchy: the bigger the network the higher up the ladder of hierarchy it sits. Thus the big multinational corporations will dominate cyberspace. And, whereas government-funded network providers offered free access, commercial providers are in the market to make profits. If cyberspace is the new gold mine, it will be exploited to the full with trade organisations dictating and shaping cyberpolicies.

Already, the really big thing on cyberspace is business: foreign trade, trillions of dollars swashing around in a hyper-paranoia of electronic transfer, chasing profit in the 24-hour global market. The Internet is becoming more and more inviting to business interests and within a few years it will become the vehicle for shopping and other forms of consumerism. Today, one can't log on to a commercial network like Compuserve without receiving an invitation to visit the 'Shopping Mall'. Soon, in the not too distant future, we will all be as the family Robinson: the bank, the post office, shopping centre, library, job centre, video store and newspapers will disappear into cyberspace and the computer, telephone, TV, VCR and stereo will all be replaced by a magic box in our living rooms. We will be logged on, tuned in and staying at home and shopping to our heart's content. Life, as they say, will never be the same again. Indeed, cyberspace has done much to boost business – trade is growing twice as fast, and foreign direct investment four times as fast, as national economies. But privatisation and deregulation means that cyberspace is a space without rules; where it can promote business, it can also advance crime.[16] Cybercrime is going to be *the* crime of the future. Organised crime is a $750-billion-a-year enterprise, the drug trafficking generates revenues of $400 billion to $500 billion; much of this money finds its way into cyberspace, where it is totally out of governments' control, where it can lose itself in split-second deals, and where it is legitimised by the international movement of more than $1 trillion a day. Within ten years it will become well nigh impossible to trace ill-gotten revenues, giving organised crime an unparalleled boost. 'Currency collapse' from dirty cybermoney is something that even gives that gung-ho bible of cyberspace, *Wired*, the 'creeps'. It is one of the ten technological developments on 'The Wired Scared Shitlist': 'corrupted currency destroys global markets'.[17]

Cyberspace frontier, then, is set to follow the patterns of the old West. And like the old West, it is a terrain where marshalls and lawmen roam freely bringing order and justice whenever and wherever they can. The lawmen of cyberspace and the new heroes of the West are hackers, whiz-kids who break into computers, punish those who break the code of 'Netiquette' and terrorise other users. While hackers are lonely and social inadequates who can relate only to computers,[18] films like *Sneakers* and *Hackers* have turned them into champions of the electronic frontier. 'A Magna Carta for the Knowledge Age' describes them as heroic individuals 'who ignored every social pressure and violated every rule to develop a set of skills through an early and intense exposure to low-cost, ubiquitous computing' (so did Billy the Kid, but in his days the new technology came in the form of repeater revolvers) and who created 'new wealth in the form of the baby business that has given America the lead in cyberspatial exploration and settlement'. But not all hackers have created wealth; quite a few have created crime and have led the way for total demolition of privacy. Cellular phone (which give off signals even when they are switched off) hackers can tap into any conversation and trace anyone almost anywhere. But with or without cellular phones, soon there will be 'nowhere to hide'.[19]

Almost every computer transaction would be hacked, every conversation amenable to tapping, and mountains of personal data about individuals routinely collected, such as medical history and financial records, would be available to anyone who wants it. Online terrorism is not too far away and most of the early proponents of this sick art are hackers.[20] While some hackers will be causing increasing havoc, other hackers will be tracking them down.

The Others are on the Other Side of (Actual) Reality

One of the most pernicious myths about the Internet is that it provides free access to all the information about everything to everybody everywhere at any time. To begin with, access to the Internet is not free. Individuals working in organisations, universities and research institutions have 'free' access because their institutions pay. For individuals without institutional support, Internet access is an expensive luxury: there is the cost of the computer and necessary peripherals (£2000/$3200, recurring every two years as both the hardware and software become useless within that period); payment to the Internet provider (£180/c.$300 per year) and the telephone bills (around £500/$800 a year). One can feed a family of four in Bangladesh for a whole year for that sort of money. Thus the Internet is only available to those who can afford a computer and the connection and telephone charges that go with it. In the West, this means educated households with incomes in the upper brackets. In the US, for example, households with incomes above $75,000 are three times more likely to own a computer than households with incomes between $25,000 and $30,000.[21] That leaves most of the households of minorities in the cold. (But Asian and Pacific Islanders are more likely than whites to own a home

computer and therefore have access to the Internet.) In the Third
World – that is, countries *with* telecommunication infrastructures
– only the reasonably well-off can afford access to the Internet.
That leaves most of humanity at the mercy of real reality.[22] Contrary
to popular belief, computers are not becoming cheaper. It is true
that the price of computing power falls by half every two years. But
as soon as the price of a model falls, its production is discontinued
and manufacturers move to higher specification machines to keep
their profits growing. In any case, new software does not run on
the cheaper (lower specification) models; consumers have no option
but to upgrade. So the presumption that the average citizen can
purchase increasingly sophisticated computers at a decreasing price
is a gigantic myth. Neither is information on the Net free. Much
of it, really useful stuff from the Pentagon to research on advanced
commercial technologies is encoded. Not all the information in
the world is on the Net (thank God for that); and unless all the
world's cultures are willing to be digitised, it will never be so. The
Net, in fact, provides us with a grotesque soup of information:
statistics, data and chatter from the military, academia, research
institutions, purveyors of pornography, addicts of Western pop
music and culture, right-wing extremists, lunatics who go on about
aliens, pedophiles and all those contemplating sex with a donkey.
A great deal of this stuff is obscene; much of it is local; most of it
is deafening noise. Our attention is constantly being attracted by
someone trying to sell us something we don't want, some pervert
exhibiting his perversion, groups of cyberfreaks giggling in the
corner, while giant corporations trade gigabytes of information
about money and death.

So most of the people on the Internet are white, upper and
middle-class Americans and Europeans; and most of them are
men. Indeed, women are conspicuous largely by their absence: less
than one per cent of the people online are women. This is not
surprising: cyberspace, like earthspace, has not really been developed
with women in mind. The binary coding of cyberspace carries with
it another type of encoding: that of gender relations. Most video
games are designed with a very white, Western male view of what
children find interesting: killing, shooting and blowing things up.
In games like 'Mortal Kombat' and 'Comanche Maximum
Overkill', which contain horrific scenes of violence, the object is
simply to kill or hunt your opponent; 'Doom' and its various sequels
involve nothing more than relentless and perpetual digital killing.
The women in these games, if there are any, are either simply cyber-
bimbos, electronic renderings of Barbie dolls, or are as psychotic
as the male characters. In most cases, however, female characters
are as absent from these narratives as women from the Internet;

at best, they are there to be rescued from evil villains, as in 'Prince of Persia' and its sequel. Given this background, it is not surprising that women have not taken to cyberspace.

The cyberspace is inhabited not just by the white, middle-class male, but a *particular* type of white, middle-class male – or more appropriately two main types of white, middle-class males. The first and the most predominant type of male on cyberspace is the college student.[23] Seven out of ten institutes of higher learning in the United States provide free Internet access to their students. Apart from spending most of their time 'netsurfing', game-playing, chatting online, these students also create 'home pages' as advertisements for themselves. There are countless such home pages on the World Wide Web containing 'information' on what they eat and excrete, what they would look like if they were Martians, and their musings on God, Hegel, Chicago Bears and the Grateful Dead. When they get bored they create such home pages as 'Nymphomania' (brainchild of a Duke University freshman) or simply put pornographic pictures on their servers. When they get really bored, they write stories: the case of Joe Baker, a 21-year-old sophomore at the University of Michigan's College of Literature, Science and Arts, is only one example – the Net is full of them. In February 1995, Baker posted a story to the Usenet newsgroup alt.sex.stories in which he graphically described kidnapping and torturing one of his fellow students. In a later E-mail correspondence, Baker even described how he was going to carry out his fantasy.[24] This group of Internet users has the same demographic profile as *Playboy* readers: that is, both groups are aged 18 to 35, 80 to 90 per cent are male, they are well-educated and have a higher than average income.[25]

The 10 to 20 per cent of white, male Internet users that fall outside the *Playboy* demographic profile – they have just as high levels of income but are, perhaps, not that well-educated – are the kind of individuals who, in the days of the Empire, were rounded up and shipped off to Australia, the 'New World' or some other part of 'the colonies' to murder, rape, sodomise or otherwise tame and civilise the natives. In the new frontier that is cyberspace, these people are forging digital colonies on behalf of the Western civilisation. Frankly, many of these individuals are genuinely psychotic; real projections of the holographic Slash Gallagher, they live on various home pages maintained by numerous right-wing militia groups or belong to newsgroups like 'alt.sex.amputee' and 'alt.sex.nasal hair'. These are the kind of individuals who, hours after the recent bombing in Oklahoma City, posted diagrams explaining how to make bombs similar to the lethal mixture that blew up the Alfred Murrah federal building, with the message: 'There you go ... Thought that might help some of you'. Or the

kind of individuals who regularly post 'stories' that explain the best
way of kidnapping children and how to torture, mutilate and
sodomise them, and the best way of 'snuffing' (murdering) them.
There is an abundance of this kind of stuff on some 60 Internet
newsgroups whose titles begin with 'alt.sex.' and literally thousands
of privately run bulletin boards which pander to such horrors in
the name of freedom of expression.

One of the oldest and best-known bulletin boards is the Well,
which was established by the founders of the 'hippie' journal *Whole
Earth Review* (formerly, *Co-Evolution Quarterly*). Here's a subscriber
to the 'Well community' giving his reasons for resigning his
membership:

> Racism, sexism, and pedophilia are alive and vigorously
> protected by the subscribers. 'Jokes' about sex with 3- and 8-
> year-old children are available to anyone who cares to log on
> the Well – including your children. When I asked that such
> graffiti be placed in a less public conference, the outrage came
> in surprising salvos, including from Howard (Rheingold), who
> went on to discuss 'First Amendment Rights' – and to leave the
> 'jokes' online, no restrictions. It was explained to me that, 'after
> all, the material was labeled "Sick and Disgusting"' – I had been
> warned. From his safely isolated keyboard another told me, 'if
> you can't take a joke then FUCK YOU!' ... I try to imagine
> what a battered woman or a victim of sexual abuse feels when
> such material scrolls into view. I prefer bigots face-to-face as
> opposed to some computer-hooded adolescent scribbling on
> cyberspace toilet walls.[26]

The problem is that that half of cyberspace which is not
commercial is largely 'toilet wall'. On alt.sex.stories, for example,
you can read stories about how infant girls have their nipples cut
and throats slashed; tales of fathers sodomising their baby daughters;
mothers performing fellatio on their juvenile sons. Even in the less
psychotic arena of the alt.sex colony, sex is just another blood sport,
like killing Nazi Germans in 'Doom' or shooting hostile aliens in
'Daedalus Encounter'. It has nothing to do with intimacy,
tenderness or any other human emotion. Just what is going on in
the mind of the individual who wants to place digitised sound
samples of his sexual encounter on the Internet? Or what kind of
humanity is embodied in a person who provides an informed
description, on alt.sex.bestiality, of how to mount a horse?
Unfortunately, there *are* a lot of these people on the Internet – all
hyper-ventilating, hyper-abusing, hyper-self-abusing, sitting alone
in front of their computer screens 'chatting' to people they have
never met and are unlikely ever to meet, projecting their darker
side on the hypertext world of cyberspace.

Give me Nothing, or Give me Something Else

Hypertext is becoming the norm in cyberspace from 'edutainment' CD-ROMs like Microsoft's *Ancient Lands* to tax-preparation programmes to the multimedia tours of DNA and Dinosaurs (as, for example, on the Field Museum of Natural History's Home Page) on the World Wide Web. One can log on to the Web and cruise for hours, jumping from page to page, subject to subject, country to country, computer to computer – 'surfin' the Net' in a frenzied journey to nowhere. It is important to appreciate that surfing is the essential metaphor here: one does not stop anywhere, one carries on at the speed of light. This is totally different from looking for information. When you need information you go directly to it; and if you do not know where it is, you use a whole array of excellent tools on the Net that can take you where the information you want resides. No, this is not about information retrieval, nor learning: one can't learn simply by perusing information, one learns by digesting it, reflecting on it, critically assimilating it; nor indeed about education. It's about boredom.

Boredom is a cultural phenomenon unique to Western culture (but now, unfortunately, being spread like a virus to non-Western cultures). Bedouins, for example, can sit for hours in the desert, feeling the ripples of time, without being bored. Traditional societies know nothing of boredom. Traditional life is a goal-orientated existence where the goals are deeply embedded in the world-view of the tradition and have real meaning for those who imbibe the tradition. It is enriched by countless face-to-face, intimate relationships, based both on extended families and communal life; personal relationships in traditional societies tend to be shared, close and intimate, leading to a host of duties and responsibilities that give orientation and meaning to individual lives. In most Third World societies, individuals and communities are normally too busy trying to survive to be bored. Boredom is a product of culture where individual and communal goals have lost all their significance and meanings, where an individual's attention span is no longer than a single frame in an MTV video: five seconds. In such a culture, one needs something different to do, something different to see, some new excitement and spectacle every other moment. Netsurfing provides just that: the exhilaration of a joyride, the spectacle of visual and audio inputs, a relief from boredom and an illusion of God-like omniscience as an added extra. But, of course, travel at such a high speed has a price. Hypertext generates hyper-individuals: rootless, without a real identity, perpetually looking for the next fix, hoping that the next page on the Web will take them to nirvana. The individual himself is reduced to hypertext: a code of information. And this process seems to be accelerating. The more we come to rely on computers, the more we use them for work, education, entertainment, communication, the more we become an extension of cyberspace. Our concerns are largely limited to discrete data or information at best. Knowledge in its true sense, let alone wisdom, never really enters the equation. We are constantly moving towards the left of the axis:

discrete data – information – knowledge – wisdom.

In the continuous tracking of cyberspace, the mind loses all sense of assimilation and synthesis as discrete data jump out at us from one page to the next, from one hyperlink to another, often without logical sequence. Human perception itself becomes discrete as we jump from page to page, here taking in a text, there listening to that sound, and over there looking at a video; everything occurring at the click of the mouse, with the speed of intuition. The individual's self is reduced to discrete bits of binary code; our humanity is digested by cyberspace.

The loss of humanity is quite evident in how the rhetoric of cyberspace is being used to give new definitions to community and identity. Cyberspace, it is argued, will provide through electronic pathways what cement roads were unable to do: connect us rather than atomise us. 'Cyberspace', says 'A Magna Carta for the Knowledge Age', 'will play an important role in knitting together the diverse communities of tomorrow, facilitating the creation of "electronic neighbourhoods" bound together not by geography but by shared interests.' Virtual communities, the mind-numbing cyber forecaster Howard Rheingold[27] announces, will bloom like wild flowers in the future and every individual will be able to choose the community or communities they want to belong to. 'You want identity?' scream Usenet groups and countless bulletin boards. 'Select from the menu and sign on!' 'Or start your own community. Create a new conference!' Cyberspace, then, is the place to discover what has escaped Western man in mundane reality: community and identity, the two prerequisites for being human. Computer networks provide the ability to transcend geography, time zones and social status and develop relationships on 'forums' and 'newsgroups'. Conferences, online chats, bulletin boards are supposed to overcome the atomism of society and lead the individual to develop the multiple bonds that urban life denies. For, out there in the real world, communities have broken down, social institutions lie derelict, family has come to mean a collection of atomised individuals thrown temporarily together by the accident of birth, cities are little more than alienating perpendicular tangles, inner cities resemble bomb sites and fear and loathing stalk the streets. But belonging and posting to a Usenet group, or logging on to a bulletin board community, confirms no more an identity than belonging to a stamp collecting club or a Morris dancing society. And what responsibilities does the 'electronic neighbourhood' place on its members? Can one simply resign one's membership from a community? And is identity simply a matter of which electronic newsgroup one belongs to? Communities are shaped by a sense of belonging to a place, a geographical location, by shared values, by common struggles, by tradition and history of a location – not by joining a group of people with common interests. On this logic, the accountants of the world will instantly be transformed into a community the moment they start a newsgroup: 'alt.accounts' (with 'alt.accounts. spreadsheets' constituting a sub-community). John Gray:

> We are who we are because of the places in which we grow up, the accents and friends we acquire by chance, the burdens we have not chosen but somehow learn to cope with. Real communities are always local – places in which people have put down roots and are willing to put up with the burdens of living together. The fantasy of virtual community is that we can enjoy the benefits of community without its burdens, without the daily effort to keep delicate human connections intact. Real communities can bear these burdens because they are embedded in particular places and evoke enduring loyalties. In cyberspace, however, there is nowhere that a sense of place can grow, and no way in which the solidarities that sustain human beings through difficult times can be forged.[28]

Real community creates context. It generates issues which arise with relations to time and space, history and contemporary circumstances, and require responsible judgement – which is why so many issues are difficult, they require balancing of opposing pressures. A cyberspace community is self-selecting, exactly what a real community is not; it is contingent and transient, depending on a shared interest of those with the attention span of a thirty-second soundbite. The essence of real community is its presumptive perpetuity – you have to worry about other people because they will always be there. In a cyberspace community you can shut people off at the click of a mouse and go elsewhere. One has therefore no responsibility of any kind. Where community has come to mean not knowing that your old neighbour has died until his or her body begins to rot and driving for miles to go to a shopping mall for essential groceries, cyberspace provides an easy simulation for the sweaty hard work required for building real communities. But virtual communities serve another purpose: they protect from the race and gender mix of real community, from the contamination of pluralism. Even when ethnic and race user groups establish themselves on the Internet, they are invisible, accessed only by others from the same backgrounds and interests. Thus the totalising online character of cyberspace ensures that the marginalised stay marginalised: the external racism of Western society is echoed in cyberspace as online monoculture. Cyberspace provides an escape from the inescapable reality of diversity in the actual world. Moreover, it fulfils the desire of community by the neat trick of labelling users with communal tags. 'In the midst of desire', writes Joe Lockard, 'we sometimes function under the conceit that if we name an object after our desire, the object is what we name it. Hard-up men buy large blow-up figures of women and hump desperately, admiring the femininity of their "girlfriends" and groaning women's names over them. But whatever their imagination, it's rubberized plastic, not a woman. Likewise, cyberspace is to community as Rubber Rita is to woman.'[29] In fact, desire is being ideologically manipulated to engender familiarity and acceptance of the hardware and software that goes to make cyberspace.

Let alone generate community, cyberspace does not even enhance communication. Listen to a news group or a bulletin board conference: are people *talking* to each other, is there real communication that transforms both the sender and the recipient, what sorts of relationships are really being forged? Is it 'discussion', or is it people shouting at each other across a crowded bazaar, or simply gang warfare?[30] Everyone on the newsgroups or bulletin boards seems to be looking for something or someone: a particular bit of information, clients, files, 'how do I do that?' or, much more frequently, 'hot' sex – 'are there any girls on this thing?' When they are not looking for something, correspondents are usually abusing each other; even serious, research-orientated newsgroups appear to be burning with 'flame' (abuse) wars. This is hardly surprising: how is it possible for people who can't even say hello to each other as the door shuts on an elevator to discuss the meaning of life over a modem with complete strangers? Just what is going on in terms of the very best in electronic communication is represented in Mark Taylor and Esa Saarinan's *Imagologies*[31] which comes complete with glowing recommendations from the high and mighty of cyber- and other intellectual spaces. A sample: 'Creates new ideas and vocabulary' says the virtual reality pioneer, Jaron Lanier; a 'profound and prescient book', declares Cornel West, the black scholar and activist; 'If you want to get a headstart on the twenty first century, *Imagologies* is required reading', announces Terry Semel, President of Warner Brothers. Taylor and Saarinan claim that they wrote their book 'for an age in which people do not have the time to write or read books' (presumably because they are too busy flaming each other on the Internet) via E-mail between the US and Finland. Their aim is to produce a new form of 'media philosophy' for the postmodern age. The book thus has no logical structure, it simply strings together musings and reflections on such topics as style, speed, virtuality, cyborgs, pedagogies and other concerns of cyber freaks in a haphazard and panicky manner. We are treated to such gems of wisdom as 'in simcult, excess becomes excessive'; 'the play of surfaces exposes depth as another surface'; 'the televisual reflects the presence of absence that is the absence of presence'; 'reality is only skin deep'; 'electricity is an occult force that is the light of the world' and 'philosophy lacks the courage to be superficial'. This is what two serious analytical philosophers were communicating to each other via E-mail, for God's sake. One liners, sub-Forest Gump textual debris, amounting to some 300 pages, all in the pretence of inventing a new paradigm for cyberspace communication. One gets better graffiti at the public convenience in Oxford Street. Is it really possible to believe that communities could grow out of such breathtaking banality? To a more discerning eye, 'electronic communities' that exist on the Internet consist of millions of isolated, insatiable, individual desires feeding blindly upon each other's dismal projections.

Apart from promoting community, cyberspace is also projected as a panacea for most of our political problems. All the problems of representative democracy are going to be solved, we are told, when everyone gets online and starts voting on everything.[32] In cyber-led society, citizens will not only be better informed but will also be able to side-step varieties of pressure groups to participate directly in decision making. For Democrat Vice-President Al Gore, the information superhighway is required 'to promote, to protect and to preserve freedom and democracy'. Speaker of the House, the arch-Republican Newt Gingrich, sees in cyberspace the beginnings of a 'virtual Congress' in which power is transferred electronically 'towards the citizens out of the Washington Beltway'.[33] 'A Magna Carta for the Knowledge Age' also presents a vision of cyberspace, 'the latest American frontier': it will empower American people through unhindered access to information. The problem with this vision is that it does not actually change the system which in fact constitutes *the* problem – it simply places its faith in information technology to make the system run more smoothly. Most democratically elected governments do what they, often ideologically, have decided to do. If cyberdemocracy could get governments to change their minds, if 'push-button voting' in 'electronic townhalls' – to use the terms of Ross Perot – could force elected representatives to listen to their constituencies, then opinion polls would be just as effective. The Western democracies are not lacking public feedback; what people lack is faith in politics, politicians and political institutions. Would electronic democracy make politicians more upright, more moral, more conscientious, more responsible? Would cyberdemocracy make the Pentagon more open and accountable to the public? Would CIA operations be open to public scrutiny? What electronic democracy offers is more of the same: more instantaneously mushrooming pressure groups, more fragmented politics, more corrupt public life. As *Time* magazine notes:

> Some of the information technologies that so pervade Washington life have not only failed to cure America's ills but actually seem to have made them worse. Intensely felt public opinion leads to the impulsive passage of dubious laws; and meanwhile, the same force fosters the gridlock that keeps the nation from balancing its budget, among other things, as a host of groups clamor to protect their benefits. In both cases, the problem is that the emerging cyberdemocracy amounts to a kind of 'hyper-democracy': a nation that, contrary to all Beltway-related stereotypes, is thoroughly plugged in to Washington – too plugged in for its own good.[34]

Citizens become no more responsible simply because they give instant opinion through cyberspace than when they decide to join a lynch mob. Cyberdemocracy is lynch law. It fosters the delusion of the frontier that you can get the laws you want – but laws are not products of individual clamour but of collective and consultative acts that have to reflect the balance of the community. To be humane, just and protective of all segments of society, laws need the context of discussion, information and testing against the needs of all – the very things you can't get from an instant reflex in cyberspace. Instant decision by cyberpolls obviates the need to understand and consider, thereby taking us further and further on the march from knowledge and wisdom.

The romantic, liberating notion of information technologies draws our attention away from its more real potential: to enslave us in its totality. Beyond the rapture of free access to unlimited information and the dream of controlling all human knowledge, lies the reciprocal threat of total organisation. All newsgroups, bulletin boards, Web pages – well, everything in cyberspace – are managed by invisible system operators (sysops) who ensure that the system runs smoothly and who hold unrestricted power to deny entry, cut, delete or censor any communication, and who observe all that is going on their system. On bigger networks, Big Sysops can not only monitor what is going on but also have the ability to intercept communications, read them and re-route them in different directions. Private E-mail is not really all that private. Those who control the system, economically, technically and politically, have access to everything on the system. Absolute Sysop holds infinite invisible power. Underneath the fabricated tranquillity of cyberspace lies the possibility of surveillance by the all-knowing, all-seeing, central network system operator. Who can handle so much power without being corrupted? The monopolistic tendencies of those who control cyberspace reflect the ethos of the East India Companies. Just like the Imperial Companies, the access providers, like Sprint and Pacific Bell, are monopolies licensed by central government with the mandate to chart new territories and are working to promote a particular world-view. And just like the companies, the access providers seek total dominion over the 'New World'. Soon, 'common carriage', the public-policy means by which free-speech principles are safeguarded, may not be all that common: privately owned carriers are not too concerned about free speech[35] – just as imperial companies were not too concerned about the rights of those they colonised. We are thus set to move from the physical colonisation of the Other to virtual colonisation of everything by virtual capitalism. Virtual capitalism is not just about profitability, it is about cynical power: *vide* Microsoft's Bill Gates's megalomaniac obsession with absolute power.[36] Virtual colonisation is the new dimension of European colonialism: 'A reinvigorated recolonization of planetary reality that reduces human and non-human matter to a spreading wake of a cosmic dust-trail in the deepest space of the blazing comet of virtual capitalism.'[37] One of the worst nightmares of *Wired* foretells of a possible future to come:

> Redmond, Wash., Noon: Jan. 20, 2001 (via *Microsoft Network*) – During swearing-in ceremonies held today on the step of Whitehouse 97 (formerly building no. 9), Microsoft Chairman Bill Gates shocked the business world by announcing a hostile takeover of every company listed on the New York and Nasdaq stock exchanges minutes before taking the oath of office as 44th president of the United States.[38]

Suicidal Twin Kills Brother by Mistake

If cyberspace is the newly discovered Other of Western civilisation, then its colonisation would not be complete without the projection of Western man's repressed sexuality and spiritual yearning on to the 'new continent'. The notion of 'free cyberspace' is nothing more than the 'virgin land' concept of the original explorers of the New World. In the days of the Empire, the colonies provided the white man with an arena to live out its wildest sexual fantasies, unrestrained and uncontrolled by the mores of European social behaviour. These fantasies were projected on the natives themselves in, for example, numerous colonial fictional and travel narratives, and generated, in the words of Rana Kabbani, a 'sense of reality in the midst of unreality'.[39] The first pictorial representations of America are of a passive female virgin figure. Eastern mysticism had an equal seductiveness – it provided an answer to arid Christianity and Western man's spiritual *Angst*. Cyberspace provides both: an arena for the projection of erotic fantasies as well as a gnostic trip.

The potential for sexual union and spiritual high is best manifested in virtual reality (VR) technologies. Virtual reality is nothing more than computer-generated, three-dimensional, simulated worlds in which individuals, geared up with suitable apparatus, can project themselves, move around, and interact directly by means of the senses. Virtual reality is a product of the collective consciousness of Western culture; it has its roots in the military, space programme, computer industry, science fiction, the arts, cyperpunk and computer hacker culture. The counterculture played a major part in its evolution and embraced it as its own; during the 1980s, cyberpunk magazine *Mondo 2000* became the main platform for VR. The old-hippie-acid gurus, like Timothy Leary, see VR as a new form of electronic LSD. Jaron Lanier (he who provided zealous endorsement for the dumbfoundly ignorant and crude tome, *Imagologies*), sees VR as the answer to 'the American stupor' or moral and spiritual crisis of Western civilisation; 'Virtual reality is the first medium to come along which doesn't narrow the human spirit' and 'all you can do is be creative in Virtual reality', he declares.[40] A blind man leading so many blind moths towards a lamp that gives no light.

What we are actually being sold by cyberpunks, the computer and entertainment industry, magazines like *Wired* and mindless hype of books like *Being Digital* by the information revolution guru Nicholas Negroponte,[41] is a designer techno Utopia. And it is a Utopia that delivers what capitalism has always promised: a world where everything is nothing more than the total embodiment of one's reflected desires. When morality and politics become meaningless, when social, cultural and environmental problems seem totally insurmountable, when injustices and oppression in actual reality become unbearable, then the seduction of the magical power of technology becomes all embracing. Cyberpunks are latter-day Utopians, the counterpart of Sir Thomas Moore, Francis Bacon, Tommaso Campanella and other European Utopians who cannibalised the ideas and cultures of the 'New Worlds' to construct their redeeming fantasies. As a subculture, the merging of bohemia with information technology, cyberpunk first appeared in the 1980s; it is basically a mutant of the drug and hippie culture of the 1960s. Just as classical Utopians envisaged that the encounter with the people of the New Worlds could produce a better society in Europe, cyberpunks believe that virtual reality will lead us to a better human understanding. And just as sixteenth and seventeenth century Utopians saw the indigenous communities of America and elsewhere as a source for discovering new styles of communal living, the cyberpunks see virtually reality as a new well of social awareness, freedom, love and spiritual enlightenment. From reshaping the realities of Others to suit Europeans, we move to a new form of technological Utopianism geared to shaping the reality inside a computer.

The fascination with virtual reality is not simply functional or even aesthetic; it is, for want of a better word, tantric. In the first instance it is purely carnal; but beyond that virtual reality holds the promise of magical sex leading to mystical rapture. Western society has always considered the body to be little more than a machine, so it is hardly surprising that it is so ready to extend its limitations by merging it with other machines. When reality becomes indistinguishable from binary code in virtual reality, then even sex and mysticism are reduced to binary communication. After all, what is sex? A simple exchange of signal blips between two genetic machines. And what is mysticism? The dance of binary codes in virtual space:

> Two men are staring into a computer screen at Apple's research and development branch. While the first, a computer nerd straight out of Central Casting, mans the keyboard, beside him sits the other, John Barlow, lyricist for the Grateful Dead, psychedelics explorer, and Wyoming rancher. They watch the colorful paisley patterns representing fractual equations swirl like the aftervisions of a psychedelic hallucination, tiny Martian colonies forming on an eerie continental coastline. The computer operator magnifies one tiny piece of the pattern, and the detail expands to occupy the entire screen. Dancing microorganisms cling to a blue coral reef. The new patterns reflect the shape of the original picture. He zooms in again and the shapes are seen again and again. A supernova explodes into weather system, then spirals back down to the pods on the leaf of a fern plant. The two men witness the creation and recreation of universes. Barlow scratches his whiskers and tips his cowboy hat. 'It's like looking at the mind of God.' The nerd corrects him: 'It is the mind of God.'[42]

The mysticisms of the Mandelbrot sets are perplexed wonders for those who have lost all connection with the natural world and spirituality, who are used to thinking of the world as a machine and have no idea what is the function of a soul. The tantric dimension of cyberspace is well captured by William Gibson, who first described the term cyberspace as a 'consensual hallucination', in his seminal novel, *Neuromancer*.[43] Case, the burnt-out, suicidal protagonist of the novel, has an intense relationship with cyberspace. For him, it is a place of ecstasy and sexual intensity, of uncontrollable desire and total submission. Ordinary experience is boring and artificial by comparison. He despairs at not being able to get back into cyberspace, of being trapped in the meat that was his body; it would amount to the Fall. Again and again, the computer wizard is obsessively driven back to the information network. He desires nothing less than to become one with cyberspace.

In direct opposition to non-Western cultures, which enhance body awareness by directing the mind towards the body in such systems as Tai chi, Yoga, Tantra and acupuncture, Western culture seeks liberation from the body by dissolving into the machine. To escape his utter loneliness, his inability to relate meaningfully to nature or other cultures, even his own society, Western man seeks union with the only thing that he sees as redemptive: technology. Postmodern relativism provides no other root for escape. Only total dissolution in his own products, in the will of his technology, can bring relief from his all-embracing solitude. This is like *fana* – the total annihilation of one's ego and self in the Will of God. 'Who are you?', they asked the Muslim Sufi al-Hallaj, when he reached the state of *fana*. 'I am the Truth', he replied. For Western man the Truth lies in the projection of his desires that shapes his technology and constitutes cyberspace. Whereas al-Hallaj sought liberation from desire, the Western man seeks enslavement to desire; whereas Western man seeks release from tradition, disciplined experiential knowledge and pursues short cuts to nirvana via drugs, borrowed gnosis and redemptive technology, al-Hallaj laboured long and hard, within tradition and disciplined experiential enquiry to reach his desired goal; whereas al-Hallaj sought annihilation of his self in a higher Being, Western man wants experiential knowledge and hence salvation through his own gadgets. Just as Western man seeks community without the burdens of belonging ('community at zero cost'), instant identity without the confinements of tradition or history, and spiritual enlightenment without the troublesome bother of believing in any thing higher than himself or his technology, he seeks sex without responsibility. The quest for absolute freedom, without any responsibilities, duties or burdens, is central to Western man's being. Cybersex promises intimacy without the necessity or even desirability of giving to another. It is a one-way street: in cyberspace you enter the simulant of your desires, you feel what she (it?) feels, she is yours but you don't belong to her, while she is your puppet you are totally free. Cybersex CD-ROMs, like *Virtual Valerie*, already offer this scenario.

Soon there will be full-scale interactive movies offering totally immersive experiences.

One potential of virtual reality is that it could make actors totally redundant; if virtual images of a herd of dinosaurs can be made to stampede across a movie screen, what barriers are there to synthesising human actors digitally as well? When the actor Brandon Lee died during the shooting of *The Crow*, the producers continued with the picture by pasting digitised images of the actor into unfinished scenes. In *In the Line of Fire*, digital sequences of Clint Eastwood (playing a CIA agent trying to protect the president) were pasted on to an old newsreel of a George Bush motorcade; in *Forest Gump*, Tom Hanks pops up digitally in a whole range of historical footage. Not just that real actors can be replaced with their virtual counterparts, but the movie itself can become an interactive experience. Interactive games like 'Under the Killing Moon', which combine live and digitised action show the future possibilities. Within a decade, one will be able to shoot/dine/sleep with Julia Roberts and/or Sylvester Stallone and have virtual reality software that allows you to design your own mate and have your way with them any way you wish.

Beyond that lies the possibility of a whole new breed of 'human': in the first instance it will be more like *Digital Man* than *Hologram Man*. Once the processor circuitry miniaturises enough, it could be put inside a tiny rice-shaped piece of biocompatible material and placed under the skin. This is happening now to identify lost cats and dogs. Soon, criminals may be tagged like that. Then children – so that those kidnapped can be traced. Then everyone. In less then a decade, nanotechnology will make it possible for micromachines to be connected directly to our body tissues, even to our brains – and cyborgs, 'the ultimate transhuman, who can choose the design, form, and substance of his/her own body', will walk the earth.[44] But holographic man is not too far off, either. Real-time holographic videos of full-colour, shaded images, which float freely in space, have already been developed 'about the size and shape of a teacup or a dumpy-looking Princess Leia'.[45] In less than 20 years, Princess Leia will grow up into a fully developed hologram person.

As they enter the virtual reality of cyberspace and become a mere extension of the machine, what still continues to be human about humans? What humanity is there in a digitalised tantric trance? How dispensable is the human in cyberspace? As the Sufi agitator and anarchist guru, Hakim Bey, argues, information-induced 'gnostic Trace accumulates very gradually (like mercury poisoning) till eventually it turns pathological'.[46] What emerges out of virtual reality is Slash Gallagher, a hologram with a body, a disturbed mind trapped in an agitated soul. Cyberspace is not a new, unknown territory; it is an artificial creation where the creator(s) and the computer already know everything – every nook and cranny, every secret behind every door. 'Remove the hidden recesses, the lure of the unknown', writes Michael Heim, 'and you also destroy the erotic urge to uncover and reach further; you destroy the source of yearning. Set up a synthetic reality, place yourself in a computer-simulated environment, and you undermine the human craving to penetrate what radically eludes you, what is novel and unpredictable. The computer God's-eye view robs you of your freedom to be fully human.'[47]

Friends, what Country is This?

The digital quest for absolute freedom ends with information, the strings of ones and zeros, taking the form of physical entity. But the personal and social relationships engendered by this entity have already been engineered by those who make the machine that makes information so palpable and those who write the software that gives it its physical attributes. Cyberspace is social engineering of the worst kind. Those who have made cyberspace inevitable have shaped its datascape with their subconscious perceptions and prejudices, conscious fantasies and fears – all of them pulled out from the dark well of colonial projections. The frontier, as Frederick Jackson Turner recast it in writings dating from 1893,[48] was merely a trick of the light to make people perceive similarity and continuity as development and change, the delusion that they had indeed a new identity. Turner's raw material was the same substance that Cristobal Colon brought to the New World, Vasco de Gama took to the East, and various colonial corporations took to India and South East Asia. The goal of getting to India and fulfilling Colon's dream was a notion alive in the minds of the founding fathers of the American Republic. The frontier was a merchant venture, just like the opening of the New World, and now cyberspace. But this venture cannot be envisioned without the context of an ideology and the mechanism of control. These, whether it be 'discovery' of the New World, the spice empires, settling the American West or cyberspace, are all the same: white supremacism, the West as the yardstick of civilisation, the divine right stuff and military force – from armed galleons to the Seventh cavalry to the armed citizenry with their right to bear arms and vote through the computer terminal. The supposed democracy of cyberspace only hands control more effectively back to a centralised élite, the ideology of the free citizen making everyone oblivious to the more enduring deep structures of control. Decentralised domination solves two problems simultaneously: it makes the new territory manageable and submissive to the structures of control while keeping the citizens happy by giving them a sense of their importance as they are being used. Thus the mythic notion of the frontier is constructed to bring the past into an organised, reinterpreted unity whose main function is to give new interpretative emphasis to desired aspects of how the dominated territory is to be controlled in the future and establish that 'progress' has been achieved.

William Gibson describes cyberspace as 'an infinite cage'.[49] The cage is the contours of the colonial history within which the darker side of the West is given an infinite reign. Manufacturing fantasies that provide escape from the injustices of the mundane world is so much easier than dealing directly with real people, with real lives, real histories and real emotions, living in their own non-programmed, real communities. Under colonialism, these fantasies framed and controlled non-Western cultures of the world. In the new colony of cyberspace, they bounce right back to surround Western man in the darkness of his own projections. Cyberspace, with its techno-Utopian ideology, is an instrument for distracting Western society from its increasing spiritual poverty, utter meaninglessness and grinding misery and inhumanity of everyday lives.

Prepare for holographic Slashers to break out of 'alt.sex.stories' and stalk the earth.

Notes

1. For a discussion of the relationship between colonisation, modernity and postmodernism, see Ziaudduin Sardar, 'Do Not Adjust Your Mind: Post-modernism, Reality and the Other', *Futures*, 25 (8), October 1993, pp. 877–93.
2. 'War in the Gulf', from Empire Software, begins with the wonderful words, 'lets go kick some ass'.
3. Chris Chesher, 'Colonizing virtual reality: construction of the discourse of virtual reality 1984–1992', *Cultronix*, vol. 1, no. 1. Online journal available from: http://english-www.hss.emu.edu/cultronix.
4. *Mondo 2000*, Summer 1990, no. 2, cover.
5. Ivan Pope, 'Public domain: cruising the wires', *The Idler*, Issue 4, April-May 1994.
6. Howard Rheingold, *Virtual Reality*, (New York, Summit, 1991), p.17.
7. Progress and Freedom Foundation, 'Cyberspace and the American Dream: A Magna Carta for the Knowledge Age', available on the World Wide Web: http://www.pff.org/.
8. For the impact of 'voyages of discovery' on Other cultures, see Zia Sardar, Merryl Wyn Davies and Ashis Nandy, *Barbaric Others: A Manifesto on Western Racism*, (London, Pluto Press, 1993).
9. Chesher, 'Colonizing virtual reality'.

10. See the seminal work by Henry Nash Smith, *Virgin Lands: The American West as Symbol and Myth*, (Cambridge, Harvard University Press, 1978).

11. Mary Fuller and Henry Jenkins, 'Nintendo and New World travel writing: a dialogue', in Steven G. Jones (ed.), *Cybersociety: Computer-Mediated Communication and Community*, (London, Sage, 1995), p. 59.

12. William A. Henry III, *In Defense of Elitism*, (New York, Doubleday, 1994). For a critique of Henry, see Ziauddin Sardar, 'Other futures: non-Western cultures in futures studies', in Richard A. Slaughter (ed.), *The Knowledge Base of Future Studies*, DDM Media Group, Hawthorn (1996).

13. Jorinde Seijdel, 'Operation re-store world', *Mediamatic*, 8 (1), pp. 1862–9.

14. Harvey P. Newquist III, 'Virtual reality's commercial reality', *Computerworld*, 26 (13), pp. 93–5 (1993).

15. Cheris Kramarae, 'A backstage critique of virtual reality', in Steven G. Jones, *Cybersociety*, p. 39.

16. Jessica Matthews, 'Dirty money is way out of control in cyberspace', *International Herald Tribune*, 26 April 1995.

17. 'The Wired Scared Shitlist', *Wired*, 3 (1), pp. 110–15 (January 1995).

18. See Bruce Sterling, *Hacker Crackdown*, (New York, Bantum, 1992).

19. Richard Lacayo, 'Individual rights: nowhere to hide', *Time*, 11 November 1991, pp. 30–3.

20. Mary Ellen Mark, 'Terror on-line', *Vogue*, January 1995 (American edition).

21. Ken Cottrill, 'Poverty of resources', *The Guardian*, On-Line Section, 30 March 1995.

22. See *The Internet and the South: Superhighway or Dirt-Track?* A Report by the Panos Institute, London, 1995.

23. Fern Shen, 'America's newest student craze? It's the Internet', *International Herald Tribune*, 27 April 1995.

24. Gilbert Yap, 'Tension on the frontier', *The Star* (Kuala Lumpur), In-Tech Section, 2 May 1995.

25. 'Playboy set to snare Internet riches', *The Independent*, 17 May 1995.

26. Letter in *Utne Reader*, No 69, May–June 1995, p. 5.

27. Howard Rheingold, *The Virtual Community*, (New York, HarperPerennial, 1993).

28. John Gray, 'The sad side of cyberspace', *The Guardian*, 10 April 1995.

29. Joe Lockard, *Bad Subjects*, 18 February 1995. Online journal available from: http://english-server.hss.cmu.edu/bs.

30. For an interesting account of online gang warfare, see Michelle Slatalla and Joshua Quitner, *Masters of Deception: The Gang That Ruled Cyberspace*, (New York, Harper-Collins, 1995).

31. Marck C. Taylor and Esa Saarinen, *Imagologies: Media Philosophy*, (London, Routledge, 1994).

32. See, for example, James H. Snider, 'Democracy online: tomorrow's electronic electorate', *The Futurist*, September/October 1994, pp. 15–19.

33. Robert Wright, 'Hyper democracy', *Time*, 23 January 1995, pp. 51–6.

34. *Ibid.* p. 52.
35. See Eli Noam, 'Beyond liberalisation II: the impending doom of the common carriage', *Telecommunication Policy*, 18 (6), August 1994, pp. 435–52.
36. For an antithesis to William Henry Gates's vision, see Gar Alperovitz, 'Distributing our technological inheritance', *Technological Review*, October 1994, pp. 31–6.
37. Arthur Kroker and Michael A. Weinstein, 'The political economy of virtual reality: pan-capitalism', *Ctheory*, 17 (1–2), 1994. Online journal available from: http://english-server.hss.cmu.edu/ctheory.
38. 'The Wired Scared Shitlist', *Wired* 3.
39. Rana Kabbani, *Europe's Myths of the Orient: Devise and Rule*, (London, Macmillan, 1986), p. 29.
40. Quoted by Chris Chesher, 'Colonizing virtual reality'.
41. Nicholas Negroponte, *Being Digital*, (London, Hodder and Stoughton, 1995).
42. Douglas Rushkoff, *Cyberia: Life in the Trenches of Hyperspace*, (San Francisco, Harper, 1994), p. 26.
43. William Gibson, *Neuromancer*, (London, HarperCollins, 1984).
44. Wes Thomas, 'Nanocyborgs', *Mondo 2000*, Issue 12, pp. 19–25 (there's no date on this issue; I presume cyberpunks are not too concerned about time!).
45. Negroponte, *Being Digital*, p. 125.
46. Hakim Bey, 'The information war', *Ctheory*, 18 (1), 1995. See reference 37.
47. Michael Heim, *The Metaphysics of Virtual Reality*, (Oxford, Oxford University Press, 1993), p. 105.
48. Frederick Jackson Turner, *The Significance of the Frontier in American History*, 1893.
49. William Gibson, *Mona Lisa Overdrive*, (New York, Bantam, 1988), p. 49.

CHAPTER 2

The Microcybernetic Revolution and the Dialectics of Ignorance

Jerome R. Ravetz

What sort of revolution is occurring in microcybernetics? How does it affect the economy, social and political life, and consciousness? Who is in control, if anyone? Or is it in a runaway state? What are the implications for our understanding of ourselves in relation to our creations, and for knowing and controlling our future?

Ever since its announcement several centuries ago, the idea of a 'progress' that is to be realised in the secular world has been surviving setbacks. But in recent decades, it has become impossible to sustain the confidence that our system of material production will necessarily be beneficial to humanity. First we faced the prospect of the collapse of civilisation resulting from thermonuclear war, which itself could easily have been caused by accident or misunderstanding. As that threat receded, that of 'the environment' became salient; and with causes and effects entangled and unknowable, it is not easy to be sure that any given remedy will be sufficient or even relevant. In both cases we can see an intimate but inharmonious mixture of knowledge and ignorance. The knowledge is on the technical side and the ignorance on the environmental and social. In these cases the hard, objective knowledge of the natural sciences cannot perform its traditional function as role model for the soft, subjective social and human sciences. Rather, we see that the applications of that hard knowledge, carried out in ignorance of its context, have created possibilities of self-destruction in those total societal systems at the core of which it lies.

That background prepares us for a review of the microcybernetics revolution. Here the threats, if so they be, are not so much on the plane of sheer physical destruction, as in the societal and cultural realms. The identification of causes and effects is even more difficult. And the rate of technical change is so great that its societal and cultural effects will be particularly complicated, and also quite diverse among national cultures at different stages of penetration by the new technologies. At this stage we can only identify some general outlines of the process and consider how best to think about it, and about ourselves in relation to it. This is not a comfortable position from which to start a dialogue among those who still have the Enlightenment faith in the possibility of effective planned intervention in societal affairs. But a recognition of our impotence along with our ignorance could at least provide an opening to an understanding about ourselves in relation to our creations.

What Sort of Revolution?

Unlike any other civilisation known to us, that of Europe, over the past millennium in particular, seems to be characterised by frequent drastic changes in a variety of realms of experience. The contrast with the 'ageless' Orient is doubtless overdrawn, but there does seem to be a quality of profound and irreversible change in European history, which is not matched elsewhere. Although our inherited terms for these upheavals presuppose a cyclical conception of the process ('Re-naissance', 'Re-formation', 'Re-volution'), the ideas of 'the modern' and more recently of 'progress' have imported the assumption that the change is unidirectional, irrreversible and essentially good.

As examples of this sort of epochal transformation, we can take the original events described as Renaissance and Reformation, whereby the 'Medieval' period was ended. Although the former was largely an affair of the cultural élite and the latter in many ways a mass movement, they have some structural similarities. In each case there was a wholesale rejection of intellectual and/or institutional structures which had previously been taken for granted as the only possible, indeed the only conceivable, ones. After sharp battles, involving ideas and sometimes also force, a new reality was established, in which the old order was either suppressed altogether, or survived at the price of taking on some essential attributes of its antagonist. Thus the 'scholastic' learning that was the target of the Renaissance went into decline and decay at the end of the thirteenth century, and in spite of several attempts at revival (in the late sixteenth and late nineteenth centuries), it survived only on the far margins of the 'republic of letters' that replaced it. In the Reformation, the doctrines of the formerly Universal Church went into discredit along with its organisation; heresy became schism, and each dissident tendency consolidated power around its own doctrines and structures. Only through its own 'counter'-reformation did the Catholic Church survive and maintain its power in a part of its former domain. Europe was then split, for centuries up to the present, along lines of style in religion, thought, and economy and society.

In modern Europe, 'revolutions' began with the radical and thoroughly implausible theories of Copernicus. His great astronomical book was about the cyclical movements of the heavenly bodies (now including the earth), but later the philosopher Kant referred to a 'Copernican Revolution' in the new sense. Then historians and commentators found revolutions all around, in the present and in the past; the 'Industrial Revolution' transformed the means of material production and gave rise to urban society; and the 'Scientific Revolution' of two centuries earlier was associated with the positive knowledge and the world-view that distinguish modern Europe so definitively from all other cultures. More recently, 'revolution' indicates the overthrow of some existing structures, probably with the use of force and violence (as, notoriously, in Russia in 1917); and this connotation is present even in the philosophical concept of 'scientific revolution' advanced by Thomas Kuhn.

What happens with all these assorted revolutions? Has the term become just another multi-purpose label? Does its use really tell us something about a particular process of change? In relation to microelectronics, does the present rapid and still accelerating change constitute a revolution; and if so, what are the discontinuities, which structures will be destroyed, and what sorts of new systems will emerge?

To answer such questions, we need to distinguish the different sorts of levels at which these various revolutions can occur. Some are focused on material production; thus we have the 'Neolithic' or 'agricultural' revolution identified by archaeologists, when some of mankind adopted the sort of settled existence in which the great, highly structured river-valley civilisations emerged. Close to them are the radical changes in social systems, by which we generally understand 'revolutions' today. Such changes usually need a preparation through revolutions in ideas, advanced by intellectuals and easily chronicled by scholars in retrospect. But there are also revolutions in consciousness, as the lived experience of (some significant fraction of) humanity shifts, and what had previously been real and valuable in shaping peoples' lives is no longer so. In relation to the latter concept, we can also mention the idea of a 'generation', advanced by the Spanish historian and philosopher Ortega y Gassett;[1] this is a group of people, whose birth dates might span a decade or more, but whose coming into the world was shaped by some great experience, be it the Great War, the Depression, or the 1960s.

In the days when history was widely believed to be the science which explained human affairs, there were attempts to find causal relations among the movements at these different levels, sometimes through choosing one as 'fundamental' and the others as derivative.

Now we tend to be more modest and are satisfied if we can find illuminating connections among them. We are also well aware that all these terms are best seen as ways of organising our perceptions and ideas, rather than describing scientifically tested objects existing in some way 'out there'.

Revolution at which Levels?

Let us go through the various levels we have indicated, and see how microcybernetics scores on each of them. At the level of production of material things, we can see processes of evolution, increasingly rapid, which will eventually modify everything we have been doing, but which are not likely to 'revolutionise' everything soon. There will certainly be a steady, progressive displacement of human labour, as the variety of coordinated skills and judgements are mimicked more effectively and cheaply by computers. Factories of the future will have fewer and fewer employees, but they will still be factories; and the same can be said for offices and shops. Farms might be quite transformed, if genetic engineering enables the use of cheaper substrates than spread-out natural soil. But in general, we could imagine an evolution in technology as in personal transport, from horse-drawn carriages, through horseless carriages, to automobiles. This example serves as a reminder that although there is a continuity in form and in function from copy to copy of each type of device (for which an evolutionary history of design can easily be done), the social effects of the evolved technology as a whole can be drastic. This is clear in the case of the universally diffused private automobile, so much so that we can speak of a transformation, even a revolution, of a particular aspect of living. This is an instructive example, since none of the futuristic prophecies at the turn of this century predicted such a development.

There is, however, another more radical pattern of development of technology, a good example of which is electricity. It had traditionally been an odd little phenomenon of attractions belonging to natural magic, but it gradually became assimilated to science, and through the nineteenth century received both theoretical coherence and increasing practical application. Then electro-technology, in its two roles as a means of transfer of energy and also of transfer of information, began to accomplish things that were previously difficult or unimaginable. Traditional craft production was not merely displaced, as in the earlier Industrial Revolution in manufacturing technique and organisation; it was rendered irrelevant, as totally new things and processes came into being. Radio and then television did more than facilitate the sending of messages; they became powerful instruments of the diffusion and shaping of culture.

If we are looking for revolutionary aspects of microelectronics, we therefore do better to see them emerging critically in information technology than in productive processes in general. This choice enables a connection to be made without difficulty to another level on which revolutions can be made: that of consciousness. This will be manifested in all sorts of ways, as the materials in which information is embodied become less solid, more pliable, even 'ethereal'. For a time there will certainly arise an exhilarating sense of power to all those who come upon these technologies in adult life and are competent in them; so much is accessible, so much can be searched for and located in a twinkling; so very much so that one can really experience surfing along the World Wide Web. Such fluidity is not only in the experience; the materials themselves lose the permanence of marked paper; not merely do different versions of a text flow into one another, but the survival of particular versions, dependent as they are on complex and perpetually obsolescent systems of interacting hardware and software, becomes problematic on a time-scale even of decades.

We are now in a transitional generation with microelectronics; earlier, there was an awe about 'faster than thought' machines which were generally tended by masters of esoteric skills and which were believed to be unerring. Now they have been domesticated to a great extent, and we watch them getting cheaper, quicker, more powerful and zippy, and fallible as well, without apparent end. But hard on our heels is another generation, for whom there is no wonder, but a taking for granted of the power to create patterns and sensations; this includes a large section, mainly male, of the young of the affluent classes all over the world. In relation to the nascent revolution in instruments and techniques, they are the first generation of its children. Perhaps eventually they will also find themselves wondering at the easy skills of their own children, inhabiting another new world of yet more powerful manipulations of structures and images.

Will this change in consciousness be a Good Thing? In spite of its surface banality, this question is after all what concerns us. And in this area as in others, it is all too easy to build up a compelling case on either side of the question. For example, the rise of electronic mail opens all sorts of possibilities for citizens' actions for mutual education and joint campaigning; but simultaneously it enables the fragmentation of society into isolated groups whose members communicate meaningfully only with each other. The nation-state is weakened by this expansion of electronic populism, as constituencies can mobilise instantly and inundate legislators with their opinions.[2] Also, transnational business now operates around the globe around the clock, leaving individual national governments on the sidelines. On the other hand, the state gains new powers of surveillance (especially of E-mail activism) and of control. Whether the Utopian world of home-based 'prosumers',[3] ascribed to the Tofflers, has any resemblance to a possible future, remains in doubt.

In the sphere of culture, we are only at the beginning of a great transformation of crucial elements of teaching and learning, whereby students will benefit from multimedia, interactive programs created by gifted and well-supported teachers, instead of enduring whomever is made available by the vagaries of recruitment, training and timetabling. Of course, such programs will have their own cultural costs, as they may tend to enhance skills of quick manipulation over detailed comprehension, and also contribute further to the blurring of the distinction between image and reality. For a real possibility of a revolution in consciousness we should consider the 'leisure' market, in which 'virtual' realities may come to be more real, as providers of stimulus and engagement, than the mundane sort.

The great novelty in this new technology is its operating so much at the level of consciousness. In this it marks a major discontinuity with the dominant technologies of modern European civilisation, which grew up in a historic epoch of the truncation of consciousness, to a degree that is unprecedented among all the great world cultures. The self-awareness that characterises so many novel currents of thought, notably postmodernity, is extremely uncomfortable, even threatening, to those who need to remain in (or return to) some structure of received verities, however arbitrary the personal choice may be. For those young persons who already live in an electronic future in which their parents are among the culturally disabled, their superior competence and awareness can be a sort of liberation, but with all the dangers attendant on liberty becoming licence.

Another perspective on the same technological phenomena reveals the manipulation of peoples' consciousness through technology, not merely at the level of ideas and emotions, but even at that of lived experience. This introduces what is literally a 'false consciousness' among its mass consumers, with unknown tendencies to disable them as citizens or even workers. As Nigel Clark has argued, even 'reality-testing' may need to be redefined, as the commonly experienced reality of the natural world becomes ever more mediated by high technology.[4] It may or may not be culturally significant that so many computer games invoke symbols from a pagan past; but we cannot minimise the importance of technocratic fantasy in shaping policies for industry and society, elegantly symbolised in President Regan's 'Star Wars' initiative, which narrowly escaped being resurrected by the current Leader of the House of Representatives in the US.

One could continue with all spheres of life, listing good and bad features of what is coming, endlessly and nearly pointlessly. For, the fact is, we do not know and cannot know in detail how this nascent technology will interact with the technical, social and cultural worlds that it is in process of transforming. In general, we can at best say that the great game of good and evil will be changed, so that the interactions occur along different fronts. Whether our own personal defining characteristic of the good life, individual or social, will be favourably or adversely affected out of all that, cannot be predicted from an argument conducted in such an orthodox scholastic style of pro and con. There are some trends which can be extrapolated without any apparent perturbing effects, where conclusions can be drawn with some definiteness; thus we have George Spencer's thesis on the effects of microcybernetics on production and joblessness. But in general we do better to make not so much predictions as prospective structural assessments of this ongoing revolution in this core technology of our civilisation.

Who are the 'We' who Decide?

One of the characteristic marks of technological fantasists over the ages is their lack of concern for the brutal realities of the use and control of technology. The sure sign of a fantasist is the use of the term 'we' to stand for those who will not merely benefit from, but who will also control, the new technology. In the days when the sufferers from new technologies were those already disenfranchised in one way or another, the optimistically inclusive 'we' was at least plausible; those who were in a position to imbibe the propaganda stood a fair chance of enjoying the benefits of the innovation being promoted. Things will be different now, for modern technology has blurred some of the divisions of access to power and to mainstream culture. In some cases, the victims of 'progress' may be socially indistinguishable from its perpetrators. This has been most marked in the NIMBY (Not In My Back Yard) phenomenon, where the local protesters may well be of a superior social class to the official agents or defenders of the LULU (Locally Unwanted Land Use) schemes.

In the case of microcybernetics, the structures of power, benefit and oppression are as complex and as yet ill-defined as one might expect from a nascent revolutionary technology. The struggles over the Internet are a reflection of this emerging picture. Those who have hitherto operated the system are of course in a privileged position within society; but they are sufficiently broadly based to be able to take a stand for direct democracy against either state or commercial control. And this particular system is not embedded in the sort of industry where bosses can easily command subordinates to obey orders or else be punished. It is known that the Internet got its polycentric structure in the context of threatened nuclear war; but the decentralised, nearly anarchic polity of skilled computer users have made it into a new sort of social institution, running on a consensual enlightened etiquette and ethic. In this present case, explicit external direction will be more difficult to impose than in any other technology we have known so far, because of the very widely diffused ability to modify the elements of the system or to circumvent its formal structures. The fight over the 'clipper chip', intended to provide the US government with the facility to break into any message on the Net, is an indication of the shape of this new politics. While the democratic/libertarian protest was getting under way, someone showed technically that the concept was flawed; and the whole project collapsed.

In that special area of microcybernetics, the 'highway' for messages containing information, it could be said that the power of citizens can indeed be exerted in a democratic fashion. There the 'we' has been shown to possess some reality, and indeed could be developed into ever broader constituencies through extensions to the Net. But the institutions through which hardware and software are made available to the Net are thoroughly traditional; Bill Gates of Microsoft has never pretended to be running a co-op. Also, it remains to be seen how much such benefits will be shared by groups that are less culturally privileged. Certainly, the economies of electronic transmission will enable the more privileged sectors of the less privileged societies to participate with fewer disadvantages in global intellectual culture. Whether the new technologies will enable the less privileged among the more privileged to assert themselves is another question. If nothing else, entry to the multimedia world now costs about as much as a used car.

Furthermore, microcybernetics in the home is part of the leisure industry, that large and growing sector of the economies of the still affluent societies. And it is in leisure that we see the contradiction mentioned by Vivian Sobchack,[5] that between citizens and consumers. It is not that being a consumer is necessarily a bad or degraded state; we are all consumers, some or even most of the time. But whereas a citizen debates about policies, a consumer can do no more than choose among products. A nation of consumers is one without debate, one where issues are concealed behind the given array of products and the propaganda for these. Since the leisure pursuits offered by microcybernetics increasingly tend to make artificial, commercialised realities even still more vivid than what is actually out there, the contradiction between electronically

enabled citizens and electronically disabled consumers may well
come to a head some time.

My concern here is not to strike a balance between the 'positive'
and 'negative' aspects of these new products, but only to point out
certain structural features of this new market. First, it is highly
skewed in structure, with a few mega-firms; and for them the profits
and power are enormous. Of course, computer games are only the
beginning of the multi-faceted leisure industry which is soon to be
provided via optical fibres. We can expect these to become ever
more sophisticated, realistic (like 'The Family' in *Fahrenheit 451*[6])
and also enlightened in various ways. And there will doubtless be
a large industry in 'info-' or 'edu-tainment', supplanting and perhaps
even replacing traditional methods of imparting useful information
and skills. The relevant polarities are on the individual and social
dimensions: for the individual, whether the new media enhance
activity and consciousness, or foster passivity and fantasy; and at
the social level, whether they lead to citizenship or to consumerism.
It would be naive to assume that the 'good' polarities stick together;
thus it has already been observed that bulletin boards can lead to
the splitting of society into discrete, mutually isolated groups; and
the rise of DIY pornography on a mass scale was known to have
been of great importance in the success of the French
Minitel system.

So if we are thinking about 'we' in connection with microcybernetics, our image could be either the harmoniously anarchistic
Net, or the addictive, fantasising Nintendo, or Microsoft which
will provide enablement to anything so long as it pays. One task
for us is to see which combination of these symbols are becoming
effective, in which areas, as the technology evolves.

Microcybernetics: a Runaway Technology

In some ways this is the age of societal control of technology.
Increasingly, the environmental, ethical and even societal
implications of industrial and technological developments, and
even of research, are publicly scrutinised. In this respect, there is
more democratic control over the whole scientific system than ever
before, not only in practice but also in principle. For this scrutiny
is performed by agencies and individuals outside the community
of those responsible for the work, even including some with an
announced hostility to it. Increasingly, citizens' panels modelled
on juries are convened to pass judgement on technologies, and their
opinions have a moral and political weight commensurate with those
of persons who actually know something about the issue from their
own working experience. Such external forces can now influence

the shape of work that is done in various sensitive areas; whether it be Greenpeace sponsoring the development of an eco-refrigerator, or English animal activists now gaining power to affect the style and economics of livestock farming, the power of ethical and environmental movements to change policies and change consciousness must not be underestimated.

Of course, the extent of external influence depends on many special factors, including the vulnerability of an industry and the degree of arousal of popular consciousness. Thus civil nuclear power may be a paradigm of an industry that destroyed itself on environmental grounds. The euphoria and arrogance of the early leaders of the industry, which led to popular disillusion when delays, cost overruns and eventually accidents occurred, made it politically vulnerable. And then its dependence on a very few large installations, each taking a long time to build (and subject to massive problems of cost and reliability), made it an easy target for protests of every sort. Opponents needed only to prevent a small number of projects from becoming real for the industry to experience paralysis and go into decline. The only easier case of a doomed technology was supersonic air transport, which survives now as a handful of copies of the aircraft, relics of a brilliant technological exercise that came to fruition just too late into the environmental age.

With that background, it might seem reasonable to hope that some degree of societal control of microcybernetics could be achieved. Certainly, the independence and integrity of the Net has been fought for, successfully so far, against intrusions from commerce and the state. But the achievement of effective societal control of any significant sort on this new technology seems to be a challenge that is already lost. Civil nuclear power was the easy case; biotechnology is intermediate. There, militant opposition has constrained developments in some countries, notably Germany; but so far the main effect has been to displace R&D elsewhere. There is, however, a general oversight of the more sensitive aspects of the new technology, either ethical (in the case of human reproduction engineering) or environmental. The degree to which this can be effective is an open question, particularly since there is no prospect of achieving binding international agreements on regulation.

The difficulties facing any possible regulation of microcybernetics are indicated by those already experienced with biotechnology. The devices themselves do not present easy targets for identification and possible attack, as in the case of nuclear power. Indeed, they are all over the place, and we have all come to depend on them in ways far beyond our knowing. Moreover, no product is on the market unless someone derives a benefit from it; and so here the situation is analogous to that in biomedical engineering, where any technique, however bizarre its human or ethical aspects, can be defended as bringing happiness to someone. To be sure, cultural nasties can be regulated to some extent for the protection of minors; but given the ease with which the products can be diffused, even here enforcement could be problematic. Worse yet, there is no definable issue where effect, cause and remedy can be presented in a plausible package for the mobilisation of popular support. Even on the question of the destruction of jobs, there is no way in which a line can be drawn defining the limits of development.

Even if someone were to define a threat and propose to start a campaign, they would find themselves confronting individuals commanding vast resources, and with reputations for ruthlessness even in dealings with colleagues. So in this way we are driven to an apparent paradox in the problems of control of this all-pervasive technology. While on the one hand distributing competence and political power to ever larger numbers of people, as a whole the technology has an inbuilt resistance to societal control of itself. Furthermore, the technology lends itself to surveillance, not only of citizens but of consumers, enabling a rapid response to mass desires that may eventually help to deflect recognition of societal needs. Between the individualised identification of persons, location through remote sensors, perhaps even implantation of devices in humans, and the transfer of so much power and information to private organisations,[7] it is easy to imagine a re-run of *1984* in which it will not be necessary for the Inner Party to create permanent war and artificial poverty for the maintenance of social stability. The disturbing prospect is that opposition to the microcybernetic consumerist dictatorship will then find its only effective location deep underground, in the hands of zealots or fanatics who are content to destroy without bothering to dialogue. And microcybernetic technology is particularly vulnerable to just such a sort of opposition; as we have seen, hackers generally get caught only when they become brazen; and a determined band of computer nihilists, endowed with patience as well as skill, could even now be ensconced deep in the system, planting their bugs, worms and bombs. The response of the state to such threats is inevitable: its machinery of surveillance and control would be deployed all over against the invisible enemy. Then we could encounter a political contradiction: would such a regime be consistent with the sort of diversity and innovation which is necessary for the growth and even maintenance of the highly sophisticated hard- and soft-ware technology underlying microcybernetics? The example of the Socialist countries, bereft of innovation even more than of consumer goods, is not a complete precedent, but it provides an example of stagnation and ultimate collapse in the interest of bureaucratic and societal stability.

It could be that this prediction is too gloomy and that this very warning will stimulate some who already have experience of fighting for the Net to start now to define tasks and strategies for widespread societal control. But I cannot now envisage the issues around which such struggles could be effectively organised; and so on that topic I have everything to learn. But in the absence of such a movement, we have the situation that the technology is truly in a runaway state. Whether our society will survive its impacts on employment, and our culture survive its impacts on consciousness, seem at this point to depend more on luck than on design. This threat runs parallel to that of the destruction of the natural environment by our material technology; but there at least some things (perhaps not the most effective) are being done, even though it may be too late. In this case, the question 'what is to be done?' now presents only a blank.

A New Perspective on Progress

A useful text is the logo of the (American) Policy Studies Association, which is three intersecting rings labelled 'cause', 'effect' and 'policy'. The likely message of this is that we can go from perceived effects to their ascertained causes, and thereby frame appropriate policies.[8] This is an elegant expression of the Enlightenment faith in the practical power of scientific reason, a faith of which one eventual product has been microcybernetics. Of course, in this *fin de millénaire* period, the refractory character of social institutions and societies is quite obtrusive, and true causes leading to effective social policies are not so easy to discern. It is already widely recognised to be an open question, whether our material civilisation has irreparably damaged its matrix in the global natural environment; and we cannot even be sure that we are safe from a crippling nuclear war. Now we face another open question, that is whether the social and cultural stresses and instabilities induced by microcybernetics will be too much for our inherited institutions to cope with. To raise such questions is not to condemn our civilisation, to say that we should go back to some better time, or that we should or could have taken another course of development. It is well known that great civilisations have risen and decayed in the past, in a great variety of patterns and perhaps through a greater variety of causes. If we stand outside ours and see it in the perspective of millennia, we can appreciate its unique achievements as a great experiment in world-view and society. We can try to identify those possible effects of microcybernetics which help to integrate our lives and release creative energies. But we should also try to identify those contradictions which might sap and dissipate its creative energies and move it toward decline.

What we are considering here is not something which will have a totally destructive impact at the material level, and so we should expect some interplay of the integrating and the destructive tendencies, the harmonies and the contradictions, in the total societal system as it adapts to this new technology. We might first consider the integrating tendencies. These are mainly in the area of lived experience and so are more difficult to relate to issues of power and control. To understand these, our guide is McLuhan, 'the media is the message'; not that cognitive content is irrelevant, but that the style of presentation becomes an integral part of what is conveyed.

With interactive multimedia, we can expect that the traditional hegemony of the isolated line of text as the means of instruction will be eroded; the line will not only flicker in and out at the will of the participant observer; it will be reinforced and enhanced by colour pictures, still and moving, and spoken words and music as well. We can scarcely imagine how this technology will transform the possibilities of communication and creativity for those whose sensibility is more on the aesthetic side than on the cognitive. (It will also help many to overcome the challenges presented by one or another form of disablement.) Going further, we can imagine for children at least the old distinction between work and play being overcome, as the powers of creativity inherent in the technology make every lesson an adventure. Also, with the greater engagement provided by this equipment, even the traditional content of formal education, previously learned by boring rote (and therefore accessible only to those who could endure it), could now become games. My own private fantasy is that much of standard teaching even at University level could be left to the machines, and students could then explore the human side of it all – history, literature, philosophy, whatever – either with multimedia equipment or even with a teacher.

All this is starting to happen now; and we may see it spreading soon in the two sorts of privileged learning environments: among those still advantaged and among those getting special compensation for being disadvantaged. Could we hope that such enlightening means of education (and then not restricted to the young) would diffuse throughout a society even if it were becoming gripped by problems of ever-deepening structural unemployment and the mass destruction of human values consequent on that? To escape that fate, our society would need to transform its values, so that even without a job one would still be a valued citizen, although not an effective consumer. It is just possible that the distinction could be blurred somewhat, as 'home-working' and working on contracts becomes increasingly the norm, again depending on the new technology. Then the distinction between having 'a job' and not having one would be less absolute. And those with more occasional leisure and less money would be able to make use of the economy of these media (compared to books) for their education and communication. In all such ways, one could imagine tendencies to integration, working across barriers of sensibility, age, lifestyle and income.

That optimistic vision depends on seeing citizenship as more effective than consumerism in the microcybernetic society. Now we must focus on the darker side of consumerism. Although economists generally remain in a state of blissful ignorance on this matter (as on so many others), it is no longer possible to sustain the assumption that private sector consumption is essentially of 'goods', and that any associated 'bads' are necessarily external to the transaction. The extra-legal sector of business is important in the economies of many nations, and even (on occasion) of some government agencies. A significant proportion of personal consumption is of 'drugs' requiring some sort of regulation, ranging from sugar and caffeine (unregulated) through tobacco and alcohol, and then to those declared illegal in some, most or all places. Extending this idea to services, we have such complex and contested areas as commercial sex (either in its illegal practice or its legal promotion) and even tourism. Even our diets are criticised, either for their effect on individuals' nutrition, or through their collective impact on the eco-system (as with the legendary destruction of rain forests for the sake of hamburgers). Again, this is only making explicit what was there in practice already; historians know that the earliest success of mass marketing in the US included ventures with marketing nonsense (Proctor & Gamble's Ivory Soap, 'It floats') or with drugs (Duke's cigarettes).[9] Hence we have good precedents for looking at the entirely legal and in many ways desirable products that are being offered to consumers in the new microcybernetics, and to say, 'much of this is dope'.

There is a good empirical foundation for the criticism of parts of this new range of consumer products as dope, given that so many of the advertisements for new computer games praise them for being 'addictive'. For those who are not familiar with this literature, a typical sample is the following. A review of a new game in a trade journal first praises the game, 'After about 15 minutes, ... I was hooked'. But later there is a negative comment: 'Also, the very selling point about Heretic – its realism – gives me a headache. Literally. You can get so lost in the game that you become dizzy simply following your character's descent through twisting passages and winding hallways. Finally looking up, you'll be stunned to realise that you've spent the last three hours staring at the screen, pressing your keys or turning your joystick. Just remember to take a break and now and then and come back to the real world for a bit. All in all, though, Heretic is well worth the registration price of 40 dollars.' The author did not bother to remind us that his or her children could join in at no extra cost and share the especially absorbing experience. He or she might later complain to their teacher that they seem unable to maintain an effective attention-span on materials that are less arousing, and so need edu-tainment if they are to learn anything at all.[10] To put the point in the vernacular, we may some day look back with nostalgia to when the worst that could happen to people was to be couch potatoes, for then at least they could press the mute button when someone spoke to them.

Should such consumers become workers, we can expect a more subtle contradiction to present. This was worked out early in this century in *The Machine Stopped* by E.M. Forster.[11] This is about the collapse of quality control in a high technology society; eventually the machine destroys itself. In our present terms, we may say that quality assurance requires something over and above consumerism, namely citizenship. This has been expressed most clearly in the campaigns for quality in Japanese industry; there workers are reminded that it is their duty to stop the line if defectives are going through. Of course they risk victimisation if superiors do not want to know; and so effective quality assurance requires a moral commitment right up the line, a true polity committed to excellence in the organisation. It also requires competence of a very old-fashioned sort; I have discussed this elsewhere in connection with a 'classical' style of art and work, as distinct from the 'modern' and 'post-modern'.[12] The destruction of quality assurance can thus be seen as a contradiction of any consumerist society,[13] and particularly of one where the consciousness of the consumers has been so cut adrift from reality. For without quality assurance the technological basis of the whole culture will assuredly degrade and perhaps collapse. The more sophisticated the technological system, the more critically dependent it is on the quality of its hardware and software, the less possibility there is for it to 'gently degrade' and move to a lower but still effective level of performance. It is impossible to gauge the extent to which this has already occurred. Doubtless, although nearly all hardware and most software systems work well, the catastrophic failure of many large software projects has been well chronicled;[14] and now we discover that in some cases standard chips or programs cannot be relied on even for simple arithmetic.[15]

Finally, we must consider the possibility of sabotage and terrorism as providing the only way for dissent to be expressed. One can imagine a society in which the divisive trends of the present are extrapolated; where those with more money enjoy the liberating cultural benefits of microcybernetics; those with less can still use it for education and organisation; while those with none are even more cruelly excluded from a glittering world they see all around them than at present. Should such divisions persist for some time, so that we have new generations (in that technical sense), some experiencing ever more intoxicating powers and others experiencing ever deeper hopelessness, then the vulnerability of microcybernetics to deep penetration could become a critical weakness of the whole societal and technical system. Exclusion of secret malevolence depends on constant vigilance, which requires an alert and committed workforce; but this is just what is at risk from the new addictive consumerism. Those new protesters would not need to sit down on roads, or even to plant explosives; their satisfaction could be as secret as their deeds as, through dedicated mastery of the system, they gradually and progressively disabled its essential core. Perhaps the whole system will respond by becoming as polycentric as the Net; but then that would involve a corresponding diffusion of power which, at this moment in history, is on no one's agenda.

Conclusion

Students of 'the future' have recently been learning an important lesson: the future is unlikely to be composed of elements obtained by linear extrapolation from the past and present. The world we know has experienced too many shocks and discontinuities for us to be able to trust any method which predicts or even forecasts. The microcybernetic revolution is the extreme case of change which defies prediction, and even more evades control. To disentangle the 'positive' from the 'negative' aspects of this future may involve the making of quite unreal separations. We can expect to find enhanced citizenship and enlarged consumerism, awareness and druggedness, activity and passivity, perhaps even riches and poverty, all mixed up within communities, families and individuals. It is such a state that Donna Harraway has already experienced in California and which she celebrates in her writing. This is not to say that all the world's people will join a post-hippie culture; but that the jumbling of categories previously kept tidily apart is something which we can study as a special version of what may come to us all in some degree and style.

I may of course be wrong; as in warfare, where every new offensive weapon eventually breeds defensive ones, we may find here new means of economic, social and cultural resilience in the face of the negative aspects of the new microcybernetics. I do hope so; but they will have to be new if they are to be effective, as new as the technology which is now starting to revolutionise our societies and

our lives at all levels, and so far totally out of control. The
Enlightenment vision cast the scientist as a new sort of sage; now,
as this century draws to a close, we are increasingly forced to see
him as the sorcerer's apprentice.

In beginning to frame an adequate response to this novel
predicament, I find it useful to show how my analysis is
complementary to two recent studies that see the problem in some
depth. Bruce Mazlish[16] has shown how this new technology will
produce a change of human consciousness analogous to that
wrought by Copernicus, Darwin and Freud: we are not at the
centre of the world, we are not unique in our origins, we are not
wholly rational beings, and now we can no longer make a sharp
distinction between ourselves and machines! We can now see
ourselves as coexisting, and (thanks to nanotechnology) even
interpenetrating, with that other species, still in its early stages of
evolution, which might well come to possess intellectual and other
powers that exceed our own. In some respects his study throws
light on George Spencer's analysis, for it reinforces the point that
there are no discernible limits to the process. However, Mazlish is
not concerned here about articulating the games of domestication
and parasitism, symbiosis and competition, and support and
destruction, that will surely be played out in the near and remote
future between that species and ourselves; and this is my
present concern.

My relation with the Tofflers[17] is closer and can be expressed
in a convenient conceptual language. They see clearly that the
inexorable qualitative development of the means of production will
strongly influence the mode and the social relations of production,
and indeed the whole cultural superstructure. Their concern is that
this process will be neglected until it impacts on the whole society,
and that the response to it will then be negative, driven by fear and
confusion. So they call out for some awareness that something is
really happening; and as yet they find but a limited response. In a
sense building on their analysis and its conclusions, I explore the
dialectics of this process.

My approach might be called 'the dialectics of ignorance'. Since
we know that something will certainly happen in this revolution of
revolutions, but we cannot know what, when or how, the best we
can do is to speculate on the leading contradictions, or 'fault lines'
of the social system, where the innovations will throw up problems
that the system can solve only with difficulty or not at all. We have
already seen some such fault lines. One is in the genuine 'future
shock' (thanks to the Tofflers) that ever wider sections of the
population will experience when they find themselves disabled by
their incompetence at techniques that are second nature to their
children. Analogous to this will be the new divisions between the

rich and the poor, where the poor will be steadily expanding in size and permanence, rendered totally irrelevant to the productive process, and ever more cruelly exposed to the rewards they are incapable of earning. From such a profound alienation (which might spread to some offspring of the rich and competent) there is the enhanced vulnerability of the whole system to sabotage and terrorism; and should that occur regularly, then the whole tone of civilised life would be affected for the worse. The parable of *Penguin Island*[18] is available to us here; as the descendants of the bomb-throwing anarchists of the 1890s became both more destructive and more commonplace, civilisation gradually disintegrated – and then started all over again.

As truth is the first casualty in conventional war, liberty is quickly jettisoned in the war against terrorism; and the state will be well prepared to implement total surveillance. Whether that situation will be consistent with the diversity and freedom necessary for developing and perhaps even maintaining a sophisticated cyberculture, is unknowable in advance. Then there are the contradictions which I consider inherent in microcybernetics as it has grown up in this civilisational setting. One is that between enabled participating citizens and disabled doped consumers: can people engage vigorously in electronic debate on the great issues of the day, while grazing through 500 channels of whatever-tainment? Perhaps in America they can; only time will tell. And the other inherent contradiction is that between the postmodern consciousness of virtual reality, where the external world is less interesting and real than what comes out of the goggles, and the need for classical quality control, which must be maintained in a real-reality, lest we find that *The Machine Stopped*. Also, we can speculate on the consequences of the failure to keep The Other tamed and caged, in a culture where, for the first time, 'anything goes' in mass commercialised spectacles. What it will be like for a child to grow up exposed to such experiences, and what sorts of parents they will manage to be, is something we are now beginning to learn, too late to do anything about it for the present generation.

I cannot say which, if any, of these contradictions will manifest as the main fault line at any point in time and location. Others may well appear; and in some way that I cannot now imagine, the system may resolve its leading contradictions, just as the industrial system resolved those identified by Marx, such as that of social production and individual appropriation. I did not say 'solved', for what happens in history is that the contradictions are contained, exported and transformed for the achievement of some stability for some time. The contradictions of the capitalist production system were resolved partly locally, by the gain in productivity, and partly globally, through the export of industrial poverty and wastes.

Now 'the environment' presents the leading material contradiction in that our industrial system cannot be sustainable on a global scale. On its side, the gain in productivity has led directly to microcybernetics and its characteristic fault lines. Perhaps these contradictions will be resolved, to some extent, by a transforming expansion of creativity and consciousness, as the new media lend vividness and accessibility for all to the best of our cultural productions, old and new, as well as to the worst. What could come after that, is not for us to know.

Notes

1. José Ortega y Gassett, *The Revolt of the Masses*, (Spanish Original, 1929, Madrid).
2. Robert Wright, 'Hyper Democracy', *Time*, 23 January 1995, pp. 15–21.
3. Paul Gray, 'Inside the Minds of Gingrich's Gurus', *Time*, 23 January 1995, pp. 20–1.
4. See Chapter 5.
5. See Chapter 4.
6. Ray Bradbury, *Fahrenheit 451*, (London, Hart Davis, 1954).
7. Dave Banisar, *Call for Papers Advanced Surveillance Technologies, Conference*, 25 April 1995; <banisar@epic.org>.
8. Irving Louis Horowitz, 'Policy and Causality', *Policy Studies Journal* 22/3, 1994, pp. 437–9.
9. Alfred D. Chandler, Jr., *The Visible Hand: The Managerial Revolution in American Business*, (Cambridge, Harvard University Press, 1977).
10. Joe DeRouen, 'Shareware Out There: Heretic', *Computer Currents* (Dallas Edition), 7/2, February 1995, p. 64.
11. E.M. Forster, 'The Machine Stopped', in *Collected Short Stories*, (Harmondsworth, Penguin Books, 1954).
12. S.O. Funtowicz and J.R. Ravetz, 'The Good, the True and the Post-Modern', *Futures*, 24/10, December 1992, pp. 963–74.
13. J.R. Ravetz, 'Quality in Consumerist Civilization: Ibn Khaldun Revisited', in *The Merger of Knowledge with Power*, (London, Cassell, 1990), pp. 180–98.
14. W. Wayt Gibbs, 'Software's Chronic Crisis', *Scientific American*, September 1944, pp. 72–81.
15. Morgan Frew, 'The Year in Review', *Computer Currents*, (Dallas Edition), 7/2, February 1995, pp. 28–32; 'The New Math, Part - 0.00' (about a three-year-old error in the Windows 3.1 calculator), p. 30.
16. Bruce Mazlish, *The Fourth Discontinuity: the Co-Evolution of Humans and Machines*, (New Haven, Yale University Press, 1993).
17. Alvin and Heidi Toffler, *Creating a New Civilization; The Politics of the Third Wave*, (with a foreword by Newt Gingrich) (Atlanta, Turner, 1994).
18. Anatole France, *Penguin Island*, (1st French edition 1908).

CHAPTER 3

Microcybernetics as the Meta-Technology of Pure Control

George Spencer

Previous technological revolutions have eventually created more jobs than they displaced. Can we assume that this will happen with microelectronics? Or, by its perfect embodiment of the 'control' function, does it accomplish a 'subversive enhancement' of human labour? When people are valued by their productivity, what happens to society when machines are increasingly more productive than humans?

The Problem

The world of public policy is now experiencing a peculiar contradiction between the activities and attitudes of two key sectors. At the level of general policy, structural unemployment is recognised as a serious problem, which can in the long run affect the well-being of the population and the very stability of society. Many see considerable evidence already of such effects. But at the level of individual enterprises, both technical innovation and dominant management policies are directed towards the elimination of jobs whenever possible. Of course, there is a perceived link between the phenomena at the two levels; it is argued that the combined effect of all the piecemeal increases in efficiency and productivity will both enable us to meet overseas competition and also to achieve 'growth' whereby new jobs will be created to compensate for those that are lost.

There are many historical precedents for this optimistic view. All previous industrial revolutions have involved the destruction of some trades or even of whole industries, but with the eventual benefit of a rising standard of living for an increasing population. Through shifts in the focus of manufacturing and the historically recent move to 'services,' the system of innovation and labour-saving in capitalistic economies can make claim to both historical success, and to being the only modern social system that is sustainable even in the medium run. This historical corroboration exerts enormous pressure at the general policy level to give maximum support to the efficiency gains at enterprise level, while minimising potential unemployment effects and their attendant problems.

It has not yet been seriously questioned whether there may be unique properties of the microelectronics revolution that could inhibit or prevent a repetition of this apparent self-correcting process of industrial revolutions. We have no historical experience of a new technology that failed to stimulate an overall demand which led to the creation of more jobs than it destroyed. This is partly because each such technology (say, electric power transmission or the internal combustion engine), while displacing existing forms of 'production', still required labour in sufficient quantity for its own (and attendant) processes, that its eventual expansion led to the creation of new jobs and industries. Even the earlier development of commercial computers, with its partial displacement of unskilled clerical work, involved so much expansion in other fields that the balance of jobs was probably positive.

But as microelectronics develops, it displays features that make it different from all previous technologies. These are best given foundation by an early name given to this whole area by the prophetic scientist Norbert Wiener; he called it 'cybernetics', after the Greek word for 'steering', or *control*. What makes this technology unique is not its capability for serving as 'computer', or (as in the French) 'ordinateur'. Rather, it empowers the *most general possible technology*, that which enters into the control of all processes, all other technologies, and itself. And in doing so, it displaces or transforms all other means of control, notably those involving human limbs and minds. As it grows exponentially in power and 'economy', it displaces, replaces, or 'improves' other means of control with ever greater facility. The possible limits to growth of this technology (which is so universally emplaced in all others that it deserves the term 'meta-technology') are therefore of great relevance to public policy.

As it has been conceived and as it operates, this meta-technology interacts with the assumptions that underlie our industrial/commercial complex. These assumptions constitute systems of reality and of values that are increasingly abstracted from human experience and existence. Considering the two key terms mentioned in the first paragraph, 'efficiency' is cast in terms where humans count for no more than machines or numbers; increasingly, tasks and their goals are set in purely quantitative terms, so that any specifically human contribution is defined out of existence (or certainly out of any intrinsic importance). And yet, 'productivity' retains its historical basis as the output per human operative. This would seem to go against the trend towards dehumanisation; but that is not so, because by this definition, any increase in the ratio of output per person, by *whatever* means, is portrayed as beneficial.

The most likely means, in the context of efficiency portrayed as above, is to reduce the number of human operatives for a given production level, and thus increase quantitative efficiency. In the framework conditioned by such assumptions, there is *no reason* to protest about possible consequences of the extension of microelectronics throughout the productive process in its broadest sense; indeed, there is no recognised language in which such protests could be coherently made.

To make a start on providing some appropriate language, I shall argue that a meta-technology whose effects are realised through the control level of other processes that it enters into should be called 'microcybernetics'. This makes it clear that I am considering much more than the technical details of the construction of microelectronic chips and methods of connecting them into physical processing systems. Given this definitional framework and the social/industrial/economic background sketched above, I shall argue that this interaction of a unique meta-technology with its background values produces a situation where there is *no discernible limit* to the penetration of microcybernetics, and its displacement of 'labour' throughout all processes of human activity. This provides a perspective on the high-level policy initiatives to combat structural unemployment, and it opens the question of how radical such initiatives must become if they are to have any real effect. Put crudely, we can try to make our labour as cheap as our competitors overseas, but there is no hope of making it as efficient as many processes permeated by microcybernetics already are, and as many others promise to become in a range of areas that defies quantification. And, in the context of the changing global division of labour, our chances of winning against the emerging combination of cheap labour *with* microcybernetics are not good.

In a more general perspective, I will give brief consideration to the sort of interaction with humanity that microcybernetics represents. Up to now we have had numerous models of co-evolution of 'man' and 'machine'. The tendency sketched here is of an effective reduction of human activity (and the relevant 'values') to just those dimensions which are easily replaced by new machines, which are themselves anything but just 'mechanical'. This points to a new interaction, one better described as 'subversive enhancement' of human labour, which I shall discuss later.

'Control' as a Technology; How Marx Was Nearly Right

The basic concept in microcybernetics is 'control'; and we shall give this a quite specific meaning for this argument. First, we have to imagine how its devices can operate while lacking either purposes of their own, or even informational content. For the former, we can make an analogy with people within organisations, who have traditionally been assigned tasks to accomplish, with detailed instructions for their performance. These tasks usually have no relation to their own purposes, and in the case of a refined subdivision of labour, might have no obvious relation to any purpose at all. The production line of Chaplin's *Modern Times* expressed that purposelessness with great humour and penetration. However, all tasks assigned to humans, except perhaps the most trivial, can be accomplished to greater or lesser degrees of quality, where the criteria and standards of quality are specified along with the task itself. Hence the operative must also exercise *control*, monitoring the ongoing task against the quality standards, so as to make it an acceptable example when it is completed. The task itself, and also the control operations, will be largely but incompletely specified through a set of procedural rules. Now, the volition of the operative must be engaged at least to some extent, because there is always some exercise of judgement necessary to ensure that the products will be of acceptable quality; yet the products themselves have no direct relation to his or her own human purposes. It is in this sense that modern human labour is alienated; but we are observing the extra twist that the human operative, while alienated, must also be engaged.

Accepting 'the appropriate application of control' as a valid description of the 'element' of productive processes, we can see how microcybernetics is similar to, and yet different from, human labour in a routine, stratified production system. They are similar in that tasks are accomplished to specifications set externally. But they are different in several ways. First, both the task and the control operations must be completely specified, for the microprocessor has no discretion, judgement, or volition. This is why the diffusion of devices with the general control function has come only recently; it requires enormous computing power to simulate the human functions of observation and judgement. Further, the microprocessor does not need to 'think', as its operations are all programmed in. This is not merely the truism that computers lack consciousness. It also means that the elements which the device manipulates (0s and 1s, or presences and absences of a state in a given location) do not need to have any meaning in themselves. Following the program, the microprocessor proceeds rapidly through a variety of internal states; at any stage these can be interpreted by humans in terms of information and even function, in relation to the task at hand. Indeed, these states would not even be present were it not for the humans who had set the program for the accomplishment of particular tasks; but the ascription of human properties to them is a matter of convenience.

In some respects this characteristic of abstraction from human meaning and judgement is a drawback for this technology; the requirements on computing power are enormous. Even now, at the time of writing, true 'robots' that move around the house and run errands are primitive and clumsy. But once the technology has sufficient power to operate on a given set of tasks, it reveals its strength. This showed first in routine mathematical operations, as the calculation of numerical tables for military use; in that early application, the tasks, and the associated controls, were purely conceptual. As the power of the technology increases, its capabilities for accomplishment of tasks, and exercise of control, become ever more sophisticated. Later we shall discuss what that means in terms of the potential of that technology; for the moment we want to relate this to what Marx imagined about productive labour.

At this point, we can see some resonances with what was probably the most powerful and systematic exposition of the factors related to human involvement in progressively technically-based production: that of Marx. Determined to promote the importance of 'working' people as a means to improving their (often desperate) lot, he created an economic theory in which 'labour power' is the only genuinely creative factor of production (in contrast to land or capital, as advocated by his predecessors). Even the massively increased capability for production of finished articles offered by the crude automation of the time could still be seen as depending on the people who 'looked after' the machines, by keeping them running and by handling the problems caused by their inadequacies. Without the 'hands' to operate and control them, the machines would stand idle or quickly break down.

Marx could plausibly see the source of the added value from production not in the machinery but in the human labour of manipulation and control; the machine itself was simply 'crystallised labour power', its productivity was the outcome of earlier operations by humans of manipulation and control. He then gave an explanation of poverty in terms of the labour market; human labour power being just another commodity, it sold at its minimum cost of production (human subsistence), while its products sold at their enhanced value, the difference being pocketed by the employer as 'surplus value'. Although Marx's 'labour theory of value' has not been accepted by economists, ironically it has become the implicit basis for the valuation of people, both on the labour market and then off it as well. For it is increasingly assumed that people acquire their value on the labour market only in respect of what they can contribute to the specific purposes for which their labour is bought. The wider context of human values (and valuation) which Marx strove so hard to preserve through his political struggles has been progressively diluted; in the current atmosphere of economic pressure through continuous technological innovation at (almost?) all costs, this wider human context often seems at best marginal.

However, Marx was right in focusing on some special factor relating to human involvement in productive processes. Where he was mistaken (in hindsight) was in equating this with, in effect, the simple presence of human beings in the productive process. In a similar way to many commentators in technically less developed times, he tended to take for granted the centrality of human beings in ensuring that the desired results of productive processes were achieved: in my terms, for ensuring that the appropriate forms/activities of control were applied in whatever circumstances. In the context of this analysis, it can now be seen that it was just this capability of human beings that was the vital focus of any attempt along Marx's lines to defend the value of human 'labour'. The fact that he did not characterise the capability correctly laid his analysis open to relatively easy manipulation. My comments on the literal 'devaluation' of Marx's focal principle of the unique 'value' of labour have their focus on the 'control' capabilities which people have contributed to productive processes, and from which they are now being progressively displaced by microcybernetics. Pushed far enough, this remorseless logic leads to there being no intrinsic valuation of the people themselves. It is this understanding that underpins the statement in the introduction, that humans count for no more than machines or numbers in the ruthless arena of competitive economic advantage. If appropriate control is the key to technological activity, microcybernetics is the ultimate meta-technology founded on control. And people, in a situation of increasing economic/developmental pressure, are not valued any differently from other means of production. We must ask, how far can this revolution spread?

Why 'Control' is a Meta-Technology without Discernible Limits

In order to answer the question at the end of the last section, it is necessary first to sketch an understanding of the device which underpins the whole of the microcybernetic revolution: the microprocessor. Of necessity, this will involve some technical detail, but this will be kept to a minimum. The technical basis of operation of computers/microprocessors has been covered many times in many sources with different levels of detail, illustrating the immense technical achievement that a microprocessor represents. In order to appreciate the sort of effects that such a device has when it enters into existing and new activities, it is necessary to develop a conceptual understanding of such a device as an objective-realising instrument. This understanding is necessary because objectives are the reasons for the pursuance of all technologies, and the technology of microcybernetics, powered by the microprocessor, is capable in principle, and increasingly in fact, of entering into the achievement of all objectives. I will in future describe microcybernetics as a meta-technology.

What of the microprocessor itself then? How can a device which is roughly the size of a fingernail, whose entire basis of operation consists of moving tiny amounts of electricity around in order to change the patterns of magnetic states that exist within it, have such immense effects on 'human' activity of all kinds? The first element of an answer is that, in this context, small size means almost the opposite of insignificance. There is virtually no problem in locating such a device anywhere that its 'power' is needed, and its energy consumption is proportionately tiny; ergo, there is no technical penalty from its use in almost any circumstances (other than under extreme limits of space and/or energy). But, just what is the basis of this 'power', which I earlier described as 'content-less'?

There have been hints of what this basis might be in works by experts in the field. In an article from a collection published in 1980, H. A. Simon started his explanatory statement with, 'The computer is a device endowed with powers of utmost generality for processing symbols ...'[1] and went on to give some 'technical' details of how the computer achieves such processing. However, the use of the word 'symbols' is misleading, with its danger of pandering to the misgivings many people have about the supposedly arcane inner workings of computers. A much more accurate way to appreciate the inner workings of computers (the microprocessor being the processing 'heart' of the most recent computers) is that they process *symbols of the utmost generality*.

It is in that utmost generality of the 'symbols' (representations of 'information') within a microprocessor that the utmost generality of its impact is founded. To achieve utmost generality of symbolisation necessarily implies that the form of representation used must be as abstracted as possible from any specific instances where this symbol-manipulation (information-handling) capability might be used. The form of representation most suitable for 'logical' manipulation by electronic means is just about as abstracted as symbolisation can get.

The conventional way of describing this form of representation is as a string of 1s and 0s, forming the basis of a binary numbering system. This convention only serves to obscure the present issue, since what actually exists in the microprocessor at any instant in time is an array of magnetic states which are either there or not there (represented, again conventionally, as 'on' or 'off'). It is the decision of the people designing/using the computers that these should represent 1s and 0s, since this is the first step towards using the capability of the microprocessor as the basis for quantification, and this leads on to a capability to take part in (enter into) 'useful' activity. However, it must be recognised that any particular string of 1s and 0s existing in a particular area of a microprocessor's memory can 'represent' (be translated from/to) virtually anything. Dependent on the program currently residing in the microprocessor and the framework of human/technical activities (instances of control) in which its ultimately general capability is being expressed, the same string of 1s and 0s could represent (a digitalised form of) – part of the waveform of a cardiac patient – the extension or angle of inclination of a robotic limb – 'instructions' to display a particular visual symbol on a screen as part of a computer game – the position of a Boeing 747's ailerons relative to its orientation to the horizon – and the list could be virtually endless.

It is this ultimate level of abstraction of manipulation arising from the technical basis of the microprocessor which allows it to be so immensely efficient in such manipulation: the 'instant in time' mentioned above can currently be much less than a millionth of a second in even a desktop computer. Equally, it is this level of abstraction which gives the microcybernetic meta-technology, 'powered' by the microprocessor, its ultimately general capability to enter into any or all productive processes, regardless of context. The only limits on such penetration into productive processes reside in the level of sophistication of the means which exist in any 'technical' situation to provide inputs to microprocessors and to utilise/interpret the results they produce. Since such means have been receiving enormous research and development effort ever since the potential of microcybernetics began to be apparent, they have been constantly multiplying and improving. This provision of means exerts a continual multiplier effect on the range of contents in which microcybernetics can be deployed.

The inference could be drawn from this analysis that the microprocessor operates in a chameleon-like fashion, taking on the colouring of whatever background there is, in order to blend with it. Indeed, something like this argument has been advanced by writers who suggest that being able to 'blend into' a variety of circumstances is no great threat. The true perception is that the impact of microcybernetic meta-technology is much more active than this. It is protean, a 'shape-changer' that adapts/absorbs major elements of any structure in which it operates, existing or new. More than that, its intervention is so active that it can, and does, have a protean effect on the structures themselves, progressively transforming the activities it enters into as its own capabilities expand. The only element that is so general to all technological activity as to be amenable to this protean intervention is the application of 'control' to achieve desired objectives via whatever means currently exist. And this has been the traditional 'position' of human beings in the technological enterprise.

At this point, it should be clear that attempts to compare microcybernetics with any previous major technology or 'industrial revolution' are futile; its position as meta-technology, operating exclusively at the level of control as the means of 'progressing' any and all technologies (including its own), is uniquely different from anything previous. What this means in wider social, economic (and therefore, policy) terms now requires some examination.

Quantified Values and the Destruction of Human-ness

In the time when Marx made his sustained effort to locate the source of all value in human labour, many of the people on whom his analysis was based were expected to do demanding work, in brutal conditions, over very long hours, for reward that did little more than keep them alive. For all his efforts, they seem to have been very little 'valued', in any clearly observable sense. However, over a period of roughly a hundred years from that time, across the generality of working situations, the machines used (and developed) not only had more power than human workers, they progressively performed more low-level activities (instances of control). In so doing, the machines gradually came to take over many of those elements of previously human tasks which were inherently noxious, dangerous, hot, noisy, demanding of great physical effort, etc. In parallel with this development, the relative crudeness of the 'automation' of low-level control often produced increased demands for higher level control than the automation of the time could satisfy. In a significant proportion of cases, this produced more satisfying 'human' jobs than before.

Alongside these beneficial developments, another whole range of previously existing jobs did not disappear completely, but instead moved very rapidly towards deskilling. In addition, many new jobs were deliberately framed in a repetitive, deskilled framework (conforming to the dominant methodology of division of labour/production line techniques). It was already observed, in Henry Ford's time, that the work of many people resembled more that of machines (robots?) than human beings. However, even these newly-defined deskilled tasks became (under more or less stable economic conditions) progressively much better rewarded than the labourers of Marx's time. The huge increases in economic and industrial activity arising from the deskilling-dependent methodology made this possible. This was yet another factor which

gave ever-increasing weight to not only the perceived success of
deskilling at the job-design level, but also the likely success of ever
greater abstraction in considering/planning productive processes.
Thus, productive activities came to be seen more and more as the
successful performance of a framework of specified processes
(instances of control) with no necessary reference to human
involvement as such.

There was, however, a superficially contrary influence. Within
the increasingly larger, more complex organisations, even jobs with
a limited range of activities became necessarily more formalised,
with increasing needs to link those activities into a 'written',
articulated structure. This was just as applicable in 'productive'
activities as those more clearly administrational (although the
effects sometimes became apparent on different time-scales). This
ongoing/developing need for a higher proportion of better educated
staff, combined with the greater rewards for even very limited tasks
(frameworks of defined control instances), resulted in widespread
'acceptance' of the benefits of a depersonalised, a-human
methodology. This has become increasingly apparent at all levels
in recent times, not just within the management levels using the
a-human methodology as they plan for the completion of processes,
but also among those whose working lives are most affected by
such a methodology.

The grounds for acceptance of this general methodology by
management are clear. There has been abundant demonstration
of the benefits to the efficiency and productivity of the organisation
of the approach which involves the division of labour and the
restriction of individual activities. The acceptance by 'workers'
seems to be founded mainly in the richer opportunities for
participation in economic and social activity offered by being both
better paid and better educated (compared to workers of much
earlier times). This may seem suspiciously like an 'ends justify the
means' argument; that will be considered in the concluding section.
For the present stage, its importance lies in its displacement of
human values, in their broadest sense. Marx's efforts to maintain
the primacy of human labour as the focus for the creation of value
were founded in the deeply humanistic instinct that we value people
precisely because they *are* human, demonstrated by the fact that
they express (in a sense, embody) human values. Concentrating
on their direct, often intensely physical involvement in productive
processes, he could portray this embodiment as somehow directly
imparting value(s) to the process, and thus in some 'complete' sense
expressing their value(s) through the process. He could therefore
argue that they should be correspondingly valued (rewarded) for
what they had, uniquely, contributed.

Thus, in Marx's time, the very directness of involvement of people in a high proportion of productive processes allowed him to identify the involvement as the crucial focus for the exchange of value; people received valuation (payment) in return for imparting their uniquely human value(s) to processes. Whether we now see this as naive is largely irrelevant, because the participation by people in recognised productive processes is just as vitally the focus for value-exchange now as it was then. However, there is often little opportunity for expression of wider human values within the performance of modern repetitive tasks, deliberately framed as a restricted number of individual examples of control (physical or mental). The pressure for displacement of wider personal values into economic activities/existence is therefore great, and receives encouragement from a considerable array of influences and factions; the equating of human value with economic existence is crucial to the underlying logic of a mass consumer economy.

The mass consumer economy which has developed in conjunction with the vast expansion in industrial/technical means has provided, and continues to provide, more and more opportunities for economic participation and therefore, in some sense, expression of individual values. This vast expansion has been driven by enormous increases in the measures of efficiency and productivity mentioned in the introduction. It has been widely assumed, across this developmental period, that the full range of human values could somehow be left to 'ride on the back of' the continuing, yet ever-changing focus for recognised value-exchange, human participation in useful/productive activity. Certainly, the prevailing wisdom in capitalist economies over the last 15 years or more is that maximum concentration must be maintained on that focus; other values can be properly handled/considered only if we get the one over-riding value, ever-increasing efficiency/productivity, right. The problem is that this makes the whole arena of human value(s) contingent on continued participation in activities which, historically, have been progressively framed in abstracted, a-human terms. As a result of this progression, the most human of characteristics are increasingly seen as hindrances to the planning of processes. By this reasoning then, human-ness itself (since this is uniquely 'located' in values) is cast as being contingent on the participation in recognised productive processes. That participation is now under threat on the widest possible scale from the meta-technology that realises its potential by directly absorbing the requirements for control previously met by people. Unlike in previous technological revolutions, it does so increasingly without the requirement for additional or new forms of control.

The vital step towards destruction of human-ness was already taken with the historic acceptance of the assumption that the most 'efficient' method of planning 'technological' (productive/useful) activities was to give no particular importance to human involvement in those activities. Increasingly, as techniques and technologies developed, to consider that involvement as only provisional, to be 'written out' as soon as any more quantifiably efficient means became available. At that point, the perception of technological activity (and therefore 'useful' activity) as fundamentally human was already conceptually subverted; now that the quantifiably efficient means of the meta-technology are being realised, the conceptual has become reality. The apparent strategic simplification offered by locating all effective value-exchange in the participation in recognised useful activity, with other values to be expressed by individuals using the value (reward) so acquired to realise their other values, is now seen to be a fatal flaw. When the focus for effective value-exchange goes, everything else threatens to go with it. By moving towards a simplistic quantification of values, they become open to (apparently) simple replacement as soon as the 'correct' quantitative assessments justify it; human-ness becomes irrelevant, and is destroyed by default.

The Ultimate Paradox of Microcybernetics

In order to set the background for full perception of the paradox, it is necessary to re-emphasise that microcybernetics is the technology that virtually encapsulates control. It thus provides the potential means to 'enhance' the quantifiable elements of performance of any and all activities. Microcybernetics, then, appears to offer its potential by operating at the very epicentre of capitalism, not by simply resonating with capitalist principles, but by being almost a physical realisation of the capitalist dream of 'more for less'. This, of course, is much more than just a capitalist dream, since it has deep roots in human psychology; most people, offered the means to do less than before in order to achieve the same results (objectives) as before, will eagerly adopt those means.

This focal psychological principle is present in all major systems of production, but raised almost to a level of deification within capitalism. This is because, added to its psychological persuasiveness, it has the following major prescriptive influences within capitalist economies:

- the focus for the capitalist concept of progress;
- vital to the mainstream economic theories of the last 150 years;
- the badge of a successful business, a crucial influence on stock exchange valuations; and
- the dream of every individual capitalist and/or business.

It is then perhaps not surprising that there has been little sign, at the general policy level, of anything but enthusiastic support for the maximum spread of microcybernetics. In the absence of any recognisable policy to channel (or limit?) such deployment, the choice (if such it can be called) is left to those in any particular industry/market situation; 'the market knows best' philosophy rules. The result is that, in each individual instance where more efficient microcybernetic means are offered, the combined pressure of the influences detailed above is overwhelming; no manager in a capitalist society can afford to ignore them. And, from their own (company) point of view, how can they ignore the benefits? Microcybernetic devices/systems do not generally consume the same amount of company resources as people.

Means of production which produce but do not significantly consume are, in one respect, every individual capitalist's dream, because of their effects on internal company costings. The managers involved in particular displacements of people may well regret, personally, that the jobs of those people disappear. However, the disappearance of jobs is in pursuit of the ends that have underpinned the tremendous progress and economic domination achieved, largely by capitalist societies, over the past 100 to 150 years. Those ends, of growth and prosperity, have been consistently portrayed as flowing immutably from the focal principles of efficiency and productivity. The overall historical effects of unremitting concentration on those ends cannot be gainsaid; thus, no matter how painful the particular instance of job/function replacement being considered in any individual situation, it is assumed that 'the ends justify the means' in the cause of overall economic development.

It has been possible to maintain this apparently pragmatic (if unfeeling) acceptance of 'the way things are' through all previous technological revolutions. The unique nature of microcybernetics means that this apparent pragmatism requires critical re-assessment. Indeed, in the absence of any significant policy initiatives, the collective effect of the pell-mell adoption of microcybernetic meta-technology could turn out to be a nightmare for the capitalist system as a whole.

The reason why a combination of many individual dreams can become a nightmare requires examination of what 'more for less' constitutes, in the context of the analysis so far conducted. This analysis shows that it represents more exertion/application of control for less human involvement. This takes place increasingly, apparently inexorably, and in a range of areas and activities that defies quantification. Because the meta-technology operates at the traditionally human level of control in enabling the achievement of any and all objectives, *we cannot expect to discover or design new requirements for control that only people can fulfil.* The functions previously performed by people are thus increasingly open to being taken over by microcybernetics throughout all levels of activity, organisation(s) and planning. Even creativity, as expressed through any recognisable creative process, is not exempt. Creativity, in order to be of use in productive activity, must be expressed, articulated in some formal fashion, whether written, designed visually, etc. Anybody who has seen or worked with some of the most recent computer-aided design programs can have no great confidence in the persistence of some privileged status for creative workers.

As the analysis in this chapter indicates, the performance of recognisably productive/useful functions by people forms the fundamental focus for value-exchange in capitalist economies. The more people are removed from that value-exchange process, the more people will not be operationally valued, that is, they will *not be* given an economically significant amount of money. This is not just a policy position; there is no clear precedent showing people involved in recognised work as being happy to see comparable payment given to those not so involved. The subsuming of all other human values to the value realised through productive activity is here both absorbed and expressed, in a deeply personal, psychological context.

Thus, there is mounting pressure to remove more and more people from the focus of value-exchange, while the means to achieve their removal multiply without apparent limit. The impact of this removal is twofold, both aspects being insidiously detrimental to the health of a capitalist economy. Firstly, those functions taken over by microcybernetic means will not cost the organisations involved as much as when more people were involved, otherwise the microcybernetic means would not have been adopted. This exerts an inevitable downward pressure on the cost per unit of production or service that the company needs to recover. In increasingly fierce competitive markets, this will direct comparable pressure on to the profit margins which companies hope to realise on their products/services. Put simply, they will have to sell more in order to achieve the same overall profit as before. The fewer people they employ, the greater this pressure will become; a computer does not require a living wage.

The second aspect is that caused by the lack of any organised mechanism to value people without significant participation in the productive system, or 'work'. It is not suggested here that they are not valued in any way; even those who made them redundant would hotly contest such an idea. The point is that such other types of valuation have no operational (economic) effect while people remain out of recognised work. The capitalist 'work ethic' dictates that they cannot be given enough money to be significant economic consumers. Otherwise the already familiar problems of 'poverty traps' and other disincentives to work for the lower-paid workers could grow beyond control.

The companies have to adopt microcybernetic means to remain (or become more) competitive; this almost always means fewer people required to achieve the same, or more, results. The consequent pressure on costs and profits dictates a need to sell more. Yet, the continuing adoption of microcybernetic methods results in more and more people who cannot be significant economic consumers, exerting a downward pressure on the demand for goods and services. Unlike earlier revolutionary technologies, this one will not create a demand for new forms of human labour, for it will perform an increasing proportion of all activities itself. These combined pressures will exert a continual, increasing 'leaching' tendency on the fabric of a capitalist economy, sapping its lifeblood, which is the creation and exchange of monetary value.

Here then is the ultimate paradox of microcybernetics. The enhancement of particular activities and functions that it offers seems uniquely to realise all the most cherished principles and aims of a capitalist economy; the collective realisation of the totality of all the individual enhancements is deeply subversive of the whole capitalist structure, just as the 'designing out' of people is deeply subversive of values.

Managers and companies operating at enterprise level are charged with 'keeping their eye on the ball', of maximising efficiency and profit; at policy level, administrations insist that the market(s) must be left to find their own direction by whatever means they deem most effective. In such a political/ideological near-vacuum, the reaction to the emerging problems of this meta-technology is most often to demand more and more concentration on its use, in all possible circumstances; a classic case of throwing oil on a fire.

It is going to be necessary to see through the seductive nature of the enhancements offered at enterprise level if those operating at policy level are to avoid continually fueling that fire (even if by default). Without a rigorous re-examination of the true range of effects which flow from ruthless application of a-human principles, the countless subversive instances of lowering of value will gather, combine and spread. This will continue until some threshold condition is reached (or perhaps even passed), when the combined weight of their effects will be too great to be ignored any longer. At this stage, the effects may no longer be manageable (or even containable).

It would be much preferable if the 'subversive enhancement' process could be perceived, not as inevitable, but as arising from a combination of context and assumptions. A clear-eyed look at these assumptions (even those considered privileged) might just provide a framework in which a new model of human–machine interaction could be moved towards a genuinely progressive enhancement. To be genuinely progressive, the model would have to avoid the value-paralysis of simplistic quantification of completion of processes, and ensure that the people who are supposed to be the recipients of the progress are at the centre of its concepts, theory-structure and practical expression. A daunting challenge, true, but a challenge that it would be very unwise to ignore; even worse if it were a challenge which, through a simple lack of depth of perception, was not even recognised.

Note

1. H. A. Simon, 'What Computers Mean for Man and Society', reprinted in T. Forester, (ed.) *The Microelectronic Revolution*, (Oxford, Basil Blackwell, 1980), p. 421.

CHAPTER 4

Democratic Franchise and the Electronic Frontier

Vivian Sobchack

I want to begin this chapter on the 'democratic possibilities' of electronic media technologies by focusing at some length upon the word 'franchise'. It seems to me that to make explicit the historically contradictory meaning and usage of the word is to also make explicit the irreducible correlation that forms the deep and contradictory structure of Western – and capitalist – democracies. Indeed, this contradictory structure correlates *both* the freedoms of participatory citizenship *and* the freedoms of government and commercial entitlement *as* 'democracy'.

'Franchise' has multiple meanings, some now archaic and others still in full use. Rooted in the Medieval Latin 'francus' and the French variants 'franchir', 'franche', and 'franc', all of which meant 'free', the Middle English 'franchise' has been used over the centuries, on the one hand, to denote: 1) exemption from servitude or subjection; 2) freedom from arrest, granted to fugitives in certain privileged places, or the right of asylum or sanctuary; 3) citizenship or full membership of a state or corporation; and 4) the right of voting in public elections, as well as any one of the principles of qualification for the right to vote. On the other hand, 'franchise' has also meant: 1) a right or privilege granted by the power of the monarch to any individual or group of people; 2) legal immunity or exemption from a particular burden or jurisdiction, granted to an individual or corporation; 3) the territory over which such privilege extends; and – originating in North America – 4) the powers granted by a governing body to any company set up for the public interest; and 5) the authorisation granted by a company to sell its products or services in a particular area.[1]

The relationship between the two major definitional categories of 'franchise' as individual freedom and political participation on the one hand, and exclusive corporate privilege on the other, has a historical charge specific to the American context. In relation to political franchise (the right to vote in public elections and thereby influence the public sphere), it is crucial to remember that, from the beginning of the political plurality that in colonial America began

as *these* United States and was federally synthesised as *the* United
States only after the Civil War (1861–65), the criteria for voting
rights were hotly contested and varied from state to state. Whereas
Thomas Jefferson and his radical Democrats believed that political
franchise should not depend upon the ownership of real property
(land, in this instance, its most basic form), John Adams and his
federalist supporters believed political franchise should go only to
landholders who had concrete 'investment' in the state and its
regulation. Thus, until after the Civil War when passage of the
fourteen and fifteen Amendments to the Constitution legally created
federal citizenship, different states had different criteria for granting
political franchise, some of them requiring the ownership of 'real
estate'.[2]

In relation to corporate franchise (the civic right to freely
monopolise and territorialise economic enterprise), it is important
to remember that from colonial times up until 1819, the
authorisation or charter for such a privilege was granted only by
the power of the state. These first corporations, economic historian
Charles Sellers tells us,

> were chartered to enlist private capital for such public facilities
> as bridges, turnpikes and urban water systems, with investors
> deriving their profits from tolls and user fees. Their public
> purpose also justified legislatures in granting them monopoly
> privileges as to route and location, as well as the right to seize
> private property under the state's power of eminent domain.
>
> Yet the line between public purpose and private purpose
> proved elastic. Prominent among early corporations were marine
> insurance companies and banks, serving mainly the purpose of
> merchants, while manufacturing corporations multiplied after
> 1800.[3]

In 1819, Supreme Court Chief Justice John Marshall ruled on
a case upholding the rights of a chartered private college *against*
state regulation, his decision momentous to the growing
proliferation of business corporations (formed for the 'public good',
a notion increasingly expanded to include capital gain). The ruling
reasoned that 'corporate charters, because they affected property,
were contracts and therefore inviolable by the states'; furthermore,
Marshall deemed the

> corporation ... an 'artificial being' ... endowed by law with the
> advantage of 'immortality and, if the expression be allowed,
> individuality'. These advantages were conferred to enable it 'to
> manage its own affairs, and to hold property without the
> perplexing intricacies, the hazardous and endless necessity of

perpetual conveyances for the purpose of transmitting it from hand to hand.'[4]

In essence, then, the corporation was given the legal rights of a person, although, in practice, these were conceived primarily in terms of monopoly rights. It was not until the 1830s that certain states established general laws of incorporation that made the process a civic and routine right and it is surely no accident that this was the decade that also marked a period of highly increased market expansion facilitated by the new technologies of the railroad and the telegraph – whose new material structures of spatial and temporal operation eventually forced further refinements in corporate law such as the emergence of 'limited liability' and new consideration of what constituted 'intellectual property' and 'copyright'.

In sum, the history of American democracy – indeed, its very mythos – is contained in a conflated notion of 'franchise' that brings human individual political freedom into alignment with 'individual' corporate freedom. The reality underlying this myth, however, is quite different as evidenced by a legal system that, in nineteenth century America, marked increasing divergence and contestation between private and public interests in relation to the contradictory goals of the open competition of private enterprise and the monopoly privilege of franchised corporations.[5] Nonetheless, as these interests diverged, the myth of their 'common interest' not only persisted but flourished. Thus, describing Ralph Waldo Emerson in mid-nineteenth century America (called by the press 'one of the great thinkers of the age'), Sellers describes the ideological position not only of the man, but also of the nation:

> Equating the corporation with socialist equity under the benign principle of 'association', he promised that this 'country of beginnings, of projects, of vast designs and expectations', would advance 'into a new and more excellent social state than history has every recorded.'[6]

For most Americans today, then, 'franchise' means both the right to vote in public elections (implying the right of full participatory citizenship regardless of race, gender, class and property ownership) and a privileged and exclusive corporate entity like McDonalds or the Los Angeles Rams football team (implying the right to regulate trade and hold sway over both a commercial entity and territory toward the end not of the public interest, but of maximum corporate profit). Much as in Emerson's time, however, the contradictory and competitive 'association' of these two meanings of 'franchise' does not pose a problem to many Americans – particularly those of the bourgeois middle class who are most likely to own computers and bank cards and to be fully immersed in the contemporary electronic life-world. Indeed, the dialectical contestation between the two meanings of 'franchise' is synthesised as a nationalist ideology that promotes the supposed freedom of individual, economic, and political *competition* that constitutes – and, to put it vernacularly, is 'at the heart of' – American democracy.

It is within this conception of Western democracy that our present electronic culture emerges and takes form – a conception that, from a critical perspective, can be seen as dialectically grounded in contradiction and potential inequality, and synthesised at a higher and more general level of value as 'competition'. Thus, there is every reason to expect that a 'democratic' electronic culture will manifest itself in the public sphere in a similar dialectical form. Self-contradictory, it will be *both* more *and* less (not *either* more *or* less) liberating, participatory and interactive than was the case with previous, technologically-mediated cultural forms.

I have argued elsewhere, from a phenomenological perspective, that the new electronic media have radically transformed our lived-sense of temporality, spatiality, embodiment and subjectivity.[7] However, there is no simple correspondence between the emergence of new technologies and the emergence of new cultural forms. Writing about the relationship between cultural transformation and new technologies, phenomenological historian Stephen Kern suggests that some major cultural changes can be seen as '*directly* inspired by new technology', while others occur relatively independently of technology, and still others emerge from the new technological 'metaphors and analogies' that only *indirectly* alter the structures of perceptual life and thought.[8] Furthermore, our insertion in an increasingly electronic and digitised life-world occurs in modalities that are *both* technological 'transparent' (that is, the technology is effortlessly and unproblematically 'incorporated' into our very being) *and* 'hermeneutic' (that is, the technology is seen as something other than ourselves and thus in need of interpretation). Insofar as a new technology like the computer is enabling (that is, we have one and know how to use it), it allows us seemingly 'easy access' to information and to others and we use it as an extension of ourselves, 'embodying' it. However, insofar as it is not enabling (that is, we can't afford one or don't know how to use it all that well or it will not provide us with the information we want), it presents an obstacle to 'easy access' to information to others, and we see it as a technology and a problem in need of solution. It is important to recognise here that a transparent 'embodiment relation' with technology does not necessarily lead to less progressive political thought or activity on the part of its user, nor does a more reflective and reflexive 'hermeneutic relation' with technology necessarily lead to more progressive political thought and action.[9] In general, we tend to oscillate between these two forms of relation with technology whatever our political agenda. And, in general, we also tend to view 'new' technologies hermeneutically (having not yet 'incorporated' them), seeing them to varying degrees as a 'problem'.

Lastly, our relationship to technologies that instrumentally mediate and thus transform our perception and forms of communication is further complicated by the fact that, so transformed, our perception and expression are *both* amplified *and* reduced. As phenomenologist Don Ihde points out, even our embodiment relation with technology suggests that 'transparency itself is enigmatic'.[10] That is, although the 'machine- or instrument-mediated experience' in which the instrument is taken into one's experience of bodily engaging the world, whether it be primarily kinaesthetic-tactile or the extended embodiment of sight (telescope) or sound (telephone) does 'genuinely extend intentionality into the world', this extension is not without consequence.[11] A potent example is contained in AT&T's American advertising campaign of some years ago. Its phenomenological gloss on the instrument-mediated perception of the telephone told us: 'We're the people who make the distance disappear. Reach out and touch someone.' The simultaneous amplification and reduction of the capacities of our sensorium conflated by the advertisement is both poignant and paradoxical – for, with the invention of the telephone and its amplification of the power of the human voice to carry over distance came also a reduction of our bodily capacity to 'reach out and touch' those with whom we were in communication.

Thus, in relation to the new electronic technologies that mediate our perceptual and expressive relations with others and the world, what is needed – along with reflection upon the political context in which they emerged – is a phenomenological description of their perceptual consequences. Elaborated elsewhere, here I can point to only some of these in relation to our transformed perception of temporality, spatiality, embodiment and subjectivity.

Our sense of temporality has been transformed, for example, not only by the computational 'nano-second' that eludes human comprehension and measures global banking transactions, but also by the more readily comprehended VCR that manipulates time with a button and destroys chronological linearity and teleology on a daily basis. Our sense of being able to control time instantaneously has been amplified, but consequently our valuation of the notion of temporal development has been reduced to the degree that many of us feel that we have 'no time'. We want ever faster computers so they may respond *immediately* to our desire (hence, the cyberpunk imagery of directly 'jacking in' and linking brain to computer) – computational speed, on the one hand, reducing our sense of mediation as such and, on the other, amplifying our sense of the *slowness of mediation*. Thus, the child who asks: 'Mommy, why can't we fast forward the microwave?'

Our sense of spatiality also has been transformed so that even to pose the notion of a 'public sphere' – as opposed to a 'private sphere' – is problematic in the age of electronic pervasion, whether by the TV set in the living room, the computer that compels a 'tunnel vision' and relocates us in the social space of a community that exists like Samuel Butler's *Erewhon* (the Utopian space of 'nowhere'), the surveillance camera and electronically-readable bar codes that mark our movement and our habits when we bank or shop. While our personal access to the space of others has been appreciably amplified through television and computers, our privacy has been simultaneously reduced. Given to watching screens and what they display, our sense of surface and exteriority has been amplified, while our sense of depth (a function of bodily movement) and interiority has been reduced.

The way we regard our own embodiment has also changed in a reversible responsiveness to our electronic context. Our computers can now get 'viruses' (although not Aids), while we now see ourselves as 'artificial' intelligences or cyborgs constituted, from the first, by the mediations of language and culture and second, by an increasing number of life-enhancing technological mediations such as pacemakers and other bodily prostheses. Indeed, we exercise to become 'lean, mean, machines' and increasing numbers of us have come to despise mortal flesh, to call it 'meat' or 'wetware', and dream of 'downloading' our consciousness into the Utopian, immortal memory banks of computational cyberspace. And while our capacity to roam in cognitive space and to understand our relations to others and to our artefacts as non-linear, reversible and non-hierarchical has been greatly amplified, our valuation of our physical embodiment and embeddedness in the world has been greatly reduced (with, often-times, violent consequences). In sum, electronic mediation of perception and expression has transformed the previous sense of subjective being as, a colleague puts it, 'terminal identity', that is, 'an unmistakably doubled articulation in which we find both the end of the subject and new subjectivity constructed at the computer station or television screen'.[12]

As mentioned previously, these electronic transformations of our perception and expression have occurred within a political and commercial context already realised – in the synthetic mythologising of an ideological contradiction – as 'democratically competitive'. Thus, if we look, however briefly, at various instances of the way the inherent contradictions of democratic capitalism are played out in this new electronic context, we can see the same conflicts between 'freedom' and 'privilege' embedded in the doubled meaning of 'franchise' informing not only each situation of electronic mediation, but also the very attitude of those involved in it. Furthermore, these conflicts and contradictions construct not a unified 'public sphere', but a plurality of competitive 'public spheres' in which individual and institutional 'terminal identities' may dynamically situate themselves and have several, and often conflicting, self-interests.[13] And, although it is not the focus here, we also cannot forget the 'shadow public sphere' of the electronically 'disenfranchised': those economically underprivileged citizens and businesses whose conflated rights of freedom and privilege are abrogated by virtue of their lack of access or subjection to electronic media. These latter include both the literally and metaphorically 'homeless' in our brave new world, if – phenomenologically speaking – 'home' is now where the cursor and the remote control are.

Here, however, let me touch briefly upon a single example of 'terminal identity' and its self-contradictory status, specifically that of the electronic 'media guerrilla'. These often glorified hackers, crackers, phreakers and cyberpunks share what they and their admirers see as a 'public sphere of subversion'. Their avowed 'democratic' goal is to 'set information free' and their practice is to interfere in institutional nets of communication – both messing up 'business as usual' for large corporations, government agencies and academic institutions by introducing subtle and often devastating viruses into their computer systems and by cracking into and 'opening up' their electronically classified information. In addition to these attacks against the privileged franchise of those institutions that constitute the 'traditional public sphere', hackers and crackers and cyberpunks profess to be working towards an alternative and truly democratic 'counter-public sphere' in which discriminatory markers such as race and gender and nationality would lose their meaning and power. This is the Utopian vision of 'virtual reality', the 'new frontier' that has increasingly occupied hacker dreams and rhetoric.

The contradiction between the Utopian democratic desire (and rhetoric) and the reactionary politics of these new electronic media 'guerrillas' is manifest in the first two editorials of *Mondo 2000*, a hacker/cracker/cyberpunk magazine born in 1989 in Berkeley California (the hallowed ground of American student revolt in the late 1960s and the birthplace of the Free Speech movement).[14] In its first issue, *Mondo 2000* proclaimed:

The cybernet is in place ... The old information élites are crumbling. The kids are at the controls.
This magazine is about what to do until the *millennium* comes. We're talking about Total Possibilities. Radical assaults on the

limits of biology, gravity and time. The end of artificial Scarcity. The dawn of a new humanism. High-jacking technology for personal empowerment, fun and games.[15]

The next issue, however, editorially celebrated the 'seduction' of the Soviets by 'free-wheelin' consumer hypercapitalism' and promoted saving both 'ourselves and our comrades to the East from a twenty-first century legalistic, megacorporate, one-world, peace-on-earth' society by luxuriating in 'cynicism' and 'cyber-decadence':

> Call it a hyper-hip wet dream, but the information and communications technology industry requires a new *active* consumer or it's going to stall ... This is one reason why we are amplifying the mythos of the sophisticated, high-complexity, fast lane/real-time, intelligent, active and creative hacker ... A nation of TV couch potatoes (not to mention embittered self-righteous radicals) is not going to demand access to the next generation of the extensions of man.[16]

This contradiction between the updated 1960s' Utopianism of the first issue and the cynicism and cyber-decadence of the second are resolved, however, by making cynicism itself Utopian – thus the further resolution of 1960s' countercultural 'guerrilla' political action and democratic social consciousness with a particularly privileged, selfish, consumer-oriented, technologically-dependent and male libertarianism. Envisioning themselves as individual and idiosyncratic (at the same time that a large number work in the corporate computer industry), as 'console cowboys' (there are few cowgirls), *Mondo 2000*'s writers and readers dream of bucking corporate systems, riding the electronic range, and cutting through the barbed-wire master codes to keep information (like early Western frontier water rights) free and available to all – all, that is, who have computer access and skills. Promoting a new democratic society in which everyone at every level is connected through the Internet and interactive with everyone else, hackers, crackers, and cyberpunks – despite their avowed communitarian and populist dream – have no idea of how to achieve it.

Consider the following list of hacker/cracker/cyberpunk maxims compiled by one of *Mondo 2000*'s regular contributors:

- Information wants to be free.
- Access to computers and anything which may teach you something about how the world works should be unlimited and total.
- Always yield to the hands-on imperative.
- Mistrust Authority.
- Do It Yourself.
- Fight the Power.

- Feed the noise back into the system.
- Surf the edge.[17]

This bumper-sticker libertarianism is neither progressive nor democratic. And, despite all the rhetoric of 'networking', it is hardly communitarian. The hacker/cracker/cyberpunk 'world-view' pits the individual against big government and big corporations and cannot envision more than 'small group' intervention in the public sphere – as in: 'Small groups of individual "console cowboys" can wield tremendous power over governments, corporations, etc.'[18] What precisely this power is in a constructive sense is never clearly articulated. These electronic 'guerrillas' seem in favour of a 'night-watchman' state – one that functions minimally to guarantee its franchised citizens' 'natural' rights to the 'good life'. Their ideolect is one that 'winners' in the modern world adopt and speaks to a belief in personal freedom and a faith in self-help that are grounded in privilege and the *status quo*: male privilege, white privilege.

Indeed, the rights and privilege of the 'individual' in this libertarian view of things are most openly evident in the discourse surrounding the Utopian 'public sphere' of virtual reality. Supposedly the new 'public sphere' in which people can freely – and equally – come together in consensual social interaction, the magazine's major interests in virtual reality seem to be as a 'private sphere' in which a free (from inhibition or prohibition) and (generally white) male body 'comes' in sensual – and safe – sexual intercourse with a (name the colour) female body. Thus, the increasing development (and sales) of 'cybererotic' software on this new democratic frontier.

What is also revealing about the contradictions evident in the discourse around virtual reality and its focus on sexual activity at the expense of progressive social interaction is that it foregrounds the contradiction underlying the hacker's phenomenological relationship to electronic mediation and its possibilities. While the electronic media actually do enable some forms of democratic social interaction and even, in a few cases, political action (E-mail providing the major context), the hacker is less interested in these clearly-mediated – and thus hermeneutic – forms of public interactivity than he is in achieving *complete transparency* in his electronic interaction. To paraphrase Ihde's phenomenological description of the contradiction at work here in relation to the amplification and reduction of access to the world and others that the specificity of electronic technology effects, the hacker wants the transformation of interaction that the technology allows, but he wants it *in such a way* that he is basically unaware of its presence. He wants it in such a way that it *becomes* him. This desire, Ihde points out, 'both secretly *rejects* what technologies are and overlooks the transformational effects which are necessarily tied to human–technology relations. That illusory desire belongs equally to pro- and anti-technology interpretations of technology.' Thus, the hacker 'wants what the technology gives but does not want the limits, the transformations that a technologically extended body implies.'[19] Thus *Mondo 2000*'s dizzying pro-technology rhetoric hides its anti-technology dreams and its refusal to address the hermeneutic specificities, the amplifications and reductions, of electronic interaction in the public sphere leads it to a privatisation of electronic space that corresponds to the structure of both libertarian individualism and corporate capitalism.

It is not all that peculiar, then, that in addition to its articles on 'freeing information', democracy on the Internet, and the promised Utopian interactivity of virtual reality (in which free – and safe – sex becomes the prominent incentive to its colonisation), from its inception, the pages of *Mondo 2000* prominently featured advertising. Products offered for sale ran the gamut from high-tech 'intelligence boosters', 'synchronenergizers' and virtual reality equipment to more 'funky' items that evoked the 1960s in their psychedelic and hallucinogenic promises. Furthermore, as the magazine's notoriety increased, so did the glossiness of its production and its attention to its own commercial value. Indeed, in 1992, just in time for Christmas shopping and priced at $20, came *Mondo 2000: A User's Guide to the New Edge*, an encyclopedia of cyberculture which, throughout its cross-referenced alphabetical entries, guided readers to the 'Mondo Shopping Mall'. According to its editors, the Mall afforded *access*; it was:

> an access guide to *products* – yes, things you can *buy*. Educational toys, you could call them – to advance your understanding or just seduce you into joining this cultural New Thing. *Shopping Mall?!!!!* We could have called it something less crass: maybe 'Tools for Access' ... But why be pretentious about it? We are present at the apotheosis of commercial culture. Commerce is the ocean that information swims in. And, as we shall see in the Guide, the means of exchange in commercial culture is now *pure information.*[20]

Here, the dream of democratic enfranchisement is grounded not only in the desire for free access to information and free interactive communication and social participation, but also in the desire for the freedom to buy and the freedom to sell, for a freely interactive and capitalist commerce. There is no such thing, however, as 'pure' information and 'free' access on the electronic frontier. And there is no such thing as 'free' competition in capitalist commerce. The freedom to buy and sell is regulated not only by the legal privileges or corporate enfranchisement (which includes *Mondo 2000*, its logo and its T-shirts), but also by individual naiveté or disavowal in relation to the basic and contradictory 'freedoms' and meanings of 'franchise' that are conflated as the structure of 'democracy' in Western capitalist societies. This contradiction is hardly news, and so we are seeing it transparently played out once again – albeit in new electronic contexts.

The hackers and crackers and cyberpunks whose views and utopic dreams are featured in the pages of *Mondo 2000* live out this contradiction both individually and institutionally. In off hours, they see themselves the champions of a market economy in which, as enfranchised private citizens, they can exchange commodities – here, information – of equal value. By day, however, they work for and contribute to corporate enfranchisement in a capitalist economy in which commodities – here, computer access and information – are also capital investments. The conflation of these two contradictory notions of democratic enterprise makes it no surprise that *Mondo 2000*'s readers, who fancy themselves as electronic 'guerrillas' working for democracy, are in large part:

> People in their thirties, people in the computer industry. A large portion of [the] readership is successful business people in the computer industry, and in industry in general, because industry in the United States is high-tech.[21]

What is particularly dangerous about the contemporary electronic 'guerrilla' is this conflated notion of democracy in which a deep phenomenological ambivalence towards technology and towards capitalism goes unrecognised, if not completely disavowed. The electronic 'guerrilla' – the most seemingly radical freedom fighter on the new American frontier – is hardly alone in his naiveté or disavowal. If one were to look at the Utopian discourse surrounding the projected informational superhighway (or NII as it is termed by the Clinton administration) or surrounding the democratic transformations wrought through E-mail by ordinary citizens on the Department of Defense-originated Internet, one could find the same structures of ambivalence, the same confusions and conflations.

Thus, although our modes of perception and expression, our individual and social sense of time and space and embodied subjectivity, are being radically transformed by electronic mediation, the economic and political contexts in which this transformation is occurring (and which it will affect in a variety of ways over time) constrain its radical nature and put it to the service of familiar economic and political ends.

In sum, we should not pin our political hopes for a more liberal, progressive and democratic society on the 'promise' of new electronic technologies. Rather, we should foreground how electronic mediation both phenomenologically amplifies and reduces our possibilities for social well-being, both amplifies and reduces existing contradictions in the multiple public spheres we inhabit. Rather than make up an impossible future in which technology does all the political work that properly – and presently – is the province of human beings, we should dismantle utopic scenarios surrounding technology to reveal the deep ambivalences, contradictions and conflations within them.

Notes

1. These definitions are paraphrased from *The New Shorter Oxford English Dictionary*, Vol. 1, ed. Lesley Brown (New York, Oxford University Press, 1993), p. 1019.

2. The fourteenth Amendment, passed June 1868, created overarching federal rather than state citizenship for persons born or naturalised in the United States, and the fifteenth Amendment, passed February 1870, articulated the right of US citizens to vote and further stipulated this right regardless of race, colour, or previous condition of servitude.

3. Charles Sellers, *The Market Revolution: Jacksonian America, 1815–1846*, (New York, Oxford University Press, 1994).

4. *Ibid.* p. 87.

5. For more detailed discussion of the early legal history of American corporations, see both Lawrence M. Friedman, *A History of American Law*, (New York, Simon & Schuster, 1973), pp. 157–78; 446–63, and Morton J. Horowitz, *The Transformation of American Law, 1780–1860*, (Cambridge, Harvard University Press, 1977), pp. 109–39.

6. Sellers, p. 380.

7. See the following for my elaboration on this assertion: 'The Scene of the Screen: Beitrag zu einer Phenomenologie der "Gegenwartigkeit" im Film und in den elektronischen Medien', in *Materialität der Kommunikation*, eds. Hans-Ulrich Gumbrecht and Ludwig K. Pfeiffer, (Germany, Suhrkamp-Verlag, 1988), pp. 416–28; Chapter 4 of *Screening Space: The American Science Fiction Film*, (New York, Ungar, 1987O; and Chapter 4 of *The Address of the Eye: A Phenomenology of Film Experience*, (Princeton, Princeton University Press, 1992).

8. Stephen Kern, *The Culture of Time and Space: 1880–1918*, (Cambridge, Harvard University Press, 1983), pp. 6–7.

9. For discussion of embodiment and hermeneutic relations with technology, see Don Ihde, *Technology and the Lifeworld: From Garden to Earth*, (Bloomington, Indiana University Press, 1990).

10. Don Ihde, 'The Experience of Technology', *Cultural Hermeneutics*, Vol. 2 (1974), p. 272.

11. Don Ihde, *Experimental Phenomenology: An Introduction*, (New York, Paragon Books, 1977), p. 141.

12. Scott Bukatman, *Terminal Identity: The Virtual Subject in Post-Modern Science Fiction*, (Durham, North Carolina/London, Duke University Press, 1993), p. 9.

13. For further elaboration on this notion of the plurality of institutional affiliations and competing interests common to the social individual, see Robert Meister, *Political Identity: Thinking Through Marx*, (Cambridge, MA/London, Basil Blackwell, 1990).
14. Part of the following discussion of *Mondo 2000* and its politics can be found in my 'New Age Mutant Ninja Hackers: Reading *Mondo 2000*', (Special Issue: 'Flame Wars: The Discourse of Cyberculture'), *South Atlantic Quarterly*, 92:4 (Fall 1993), pp. 569–84.
15. *Mondo 2000*, no. 1 (1989), p. 11.
16. *Mondo 2000*, no. 2 (Summer 1990), pp. 8–9.
17. Gareth Branwyn, 'Cyberpunk', in *Mondo 2000: A User's Guide to the New Edge*, eds Rudy Rucker, R.U. Sirius, and Queen Mu, (New York, Harper Books, 1992), p. 66.
18. *Ibid*.
19. Ihde, pp. 75–76.
20. R.U. Sirius, 'A User's Guide to Using This Guide', *Mondo 2000: A User's Guide*, p. 16.
21. R.U. Sirius, quoted in 'Sex, Drugs, & Cyberspace', *Express: The East Bay's Free Weekly*, 28 September 1990, p. 12.

CHAPTER 5

Earthing the Ether: The Alternating Currents of Ecology and Cyberculture

Nigel Clark

Ecology and cyberculture: two discursive formations which at first glance seem bound to incommensurate paths. The first concerns itself with all that is given and enduring, its tropisms constantly leading it back toward the deep, obdurate reality of the earth. The second relishes the ephemeral currents of the electronic ether, its attraction whatever luminous body is pulsing most brightly. One heading backwards, downwards into the substrate, the other upwards, outwards into the airwaves and onto the Infobahn. Or so it appears.

By ecology, I refer not to the subdiscipline of biology, but to the countercultural 'vision' expounded by theorists and activists who have taken on themselves the role of articulating the interests of the biosphere. The radical or 'deep' forms of ecology place their emphasis on the interconnectedness of all natural beings and processes, and take this tenet of unity or wholeness as the basis for an engagement with the contemporary human condition which is likewise all-embracing. As Anne Chisholm observed of the ecological message in the early 1970s: 'What it meant was – everything links up ... Here was a new morality, and a strategy for human survival rolled into one.'[1] From this perspective, modern Western society is premised on a cultural vision of separateness of humankind from nature, a world-view which must be overturned in order to regenerate meaningful forms of communality and environmentally benign social practices. Ecologists constitute 'nature' as a domain which is ontologically prior to that of culture, believing that it is potentially accessible to human subjects in a direct and unmediated way. Such experiences of 'being in nature' are seen to contravene the dominant construct of objectivity toward nature and in this way to act as reminders that humankind is part of a larger community of life – the basic insight needed to begin the process of socio-cultural reconstruction.

This prioritising of the bond with 'untrammelled nature' resounds in ecology's negative appraisal of most forms of mediation of experience, particularly the most recent and conspicuously 'technological' modalities. In a recent countercultural initiative, however, that which is anathema to ecologists has been elevated to a position of centrality. For those most enthralled by the latest modes of data-processing and communication – known variously as hackers, crackers, phreaks, cyberpunks and cyberians – the possibility of traversing fields of pure information takes on a similar significance to the immersion in pristine nature in the ecological world-view. 'Cyberculture', as Mark Dery defines it, is 'a far-flung, loosely knit complex of sublegitimate, alternative, and oppositional subcultures (whose common project is the subversive use of technocommodities, often framed by radical body politics).'[2]

No less than that of ecology, the world-view which seems to be crystallising around transgressive practices in the new networks enunciates a desire for radical cultural transformation. According to Douglas Rushkoff, the 'cyberian vision is a heretical negation of the rules by which Western society has chosen to organise itself'.[3] Again, the benevolent spectre of universal interconnectivity is invoked. In this context it is the structures of ownership and control of the mode of information which must be subverted, in order that human subjects might reassert their communality: the enlightening moment occurring when the illicit operator breaks through some 'artificially' imposed barrier to attain commune with other 'free agents' or with a body of data which 'wants to be liberated'.

From within both camps, the demarcation between cyberculture and ecology has been underscored. 'Eco-fundamentalism is out' proclaim the editors of the magazine *Mondo 2000*. Caricatured as 'going back to the land, growing tubers and soybeans, reading by oil lamps', the project of radical ecology is simply perceived as 'boring!'.[4] Behind such dismissals is a disdain for the closure of horizons, for the merely 'finite possibilities' to which the defenders of organic nature seem to have resigned themselves. By contrast, the digitally configured universe appears to offer unlimited prospects. Artificial life researcher Christopher Langton makes the kind of claim that is music to the enhanced auditory receptors of the cybercultural generation, when he asserts: 'It is only a matter of organisation to turn "hardware" into "wetware" (biological life) and, ultimately, for "hardware" to achieve everything that has been achieved by "wetware", and more.'[5]

While cyberculture was still in the ascendant, ecological theorists began to register their concern. For those who valorised contact with organic nature, the growing tendency to cybernetically model the external world could only be construed as a further degree of severance of humankind from the natural world, with binary code appearing as the ultimate medium for the reduction of nature into abstract, quantifiable and interchangeable units. Describing an educational computer program with which children can generate a flock of birds and put them into flight, Jeremy Rifkin emphasises its inferiority to the intimate encounter with 'real' nature. The simulation model has 'no smells or tastes, no winds or bird song, no connection with soil, water, sunlight, warmth, no real ecology ...'[6] Likewise, Theodore Roszak fears that the pervasive presence of such computer modelling will alter our perception of 'reality' itself, so that we might come to take its abstract lineaments to be the true state of things. In this way, we could forfeit what is left of our appreciation of the sensuous qualities of nature, cease to feel its continuity with our own embodied experience, and lose all sense of the complexity of relationships that bind all the parts of the natural cosmos into a unified totality. For ecological critics, then, the diffusion of digitally mediated experience threatens those precious residual encounters with organic nature, and the possibility of reconciliation which they embody. As Roszak concludes:

> It may mean far more at this juncture in history for children once again to find their kinship with the animals, every one of which, in its own inarticulate way, displays greater powers of mind than any computer can even mimic well ... How much ecological sense does it make to rush to close off what remains of that experience for children by thrusting still another mechanical device upon them?[7]

Inversions of Eden

Hacker heaven, then, sounds rather like ecological purgatory, and vice versa. But beneath the surface tension, there are some significant correspondences. As Roszak himself has pointed out, ecological and cybercultural radicalism have certain common historical derivations. At the height of the 1960s' counterculture, he reminds us, electronic technology and an immaculate nature were frequently imbricated in a single vision. The first microcomputers were developed in the small workshops of counterculturally-minded computer 'hackers' who had gathered in California in the mid-1970s, and were intended to facilitate self-reliance at a grassroots level: 'The destiny of the microcomputer was to create a global culture of electronic villages cradled in a healthy natural environment – the sort of world one found scattered through the pages of the *Whole Earth Catalog*.'[8]

In part it was the spectacular growth of these 'garage' computer firms that undermined this pastoral vision of personal computing. But what also served to dissociate the cybernetic domain from the realm of nature was the installation of networks and the growing capacity for three-dimensional digital graphics. The networking of discrete terminals helped give users the impression that they were travelling from one place to another, whilst graphical interfaces simulated the spatial arrangement of the object world on the screen, with some of the most advanced forms producing the illusion of immersion in this visual field. Singularly, or imaginatively fused, these two developments prompted computer users to conceive of the loci of processing and communication as a space in its own right. Henceforth, interest in the environment in which the computer terminal was located receded before the fascination with the environment within the computer and its extensions. In other words, the image of the machine in the garden soon faded as it became possible to imagine a garden within the machine.

As the discursive production of 'cyberspace' proceeded, so too did the concern of ecologists that organic nature had, as it were, been put out to pasture. But ironically, as the countercultural impulse recrystallised around the idea of an inhabitable but totally artifactual datascape, the new domain became host to the sort of fantasies and desires that had previously been associated with 'untrammelled' nature. While Donna Haraway proposed in her celebrated 'Cyborg Manifesto'[9] that the use of informatic technologies might make us more conscious of our non-unitary identities, imperfect systems and partial modes of connectivity, many 'cyberians' have carried on regardless in their imaginary constitution of the cybernetic sphere as the site of unimpeded communication and a renewed experience of wholeness.

Just as ecologists contend that 'once humans became agriculturists, the almost paradisiacal character of prehistory was irretrievably lost',[10] so we now hear from the 'cyberian perspective' that the 'moment when people settled down in agricultural communities was the moment when everything went wrong';[11] ecology recognises 'no firm ontological divide in the field of existence',[12] whilst in the new movement 'computer programmers and psychedelic warriors together realise that "all is one"'.[13] In short, where Haraway holds out the hope that the new ubiquity of human–computer interfaces might finally spell the end of the myth of primal unity and all the dreams of a return to the garden, both ecology and cyberculture seem intent in its perpetuation, using all the tools at their disposal.

With cyberculture acknowledging the total fabrication of its chosen realm, and ecology unregenerately committed to the 'real', the two discursive formations seem bound by a mutual inversion as they gesture towards their respective Edens. What they share is a high degree of symbolic investment in a distinctive, self-contained sphere. Like the notion of a pristine wilderness, the idea of a limitless, fully immersive cyberspace serves to separate in from out, ideal world from fallen imperfect world. In each case, the privileged zone is the sanctuary of the essential, of pure form, of the way things should be in everyday life, but are not. Because it is seen to exist before and outside representation, untrammelled nature can be taken as the repository of immutable truth. But so too can the equally mythic formation of cyberspace. As the site where every kind of message converges into the universal medium of the binary code, the datasphere is construed as the representation of all representations, the very essence of human symbolic activity. Where the everyday world is compromised by illegible signs, contested regions and exclusive zones, the ideal space – at least for those who make themselves at home there – can be experienced as pure presence, a place where the subject can attain a perfect identification with the world. For those who choose to pass into the integrated circuits of nature or cyberspace, the reward is a sensation of freedom from all culturally-imposed restraints, an expanded sense of self, a feeling of wholeness.

Despite the ostensible devotion to light speeds and push button mutability, there is a discernible will to the absolute that flows in the currents of cyberculture, a sort of unspoken hope that the fusion of enough live wires might somehow generate its own earthing. In this sense, Jurgen Habermas's diagnosis of the aesthetic movements of the early twentieth century seems even more apposite in regard to the discourses on the cybernetic: 'The new value placed on the transitory, the elusive, and the ephemeral, the very celebration of dynamism, discloses the longing for an undefiled, an immaculate and stable present', he maintains.[14] Just as the grid has been a favourite trope of the aesthetic avant-garde, so too does it resound as a metaphor for the cybernetic system in the discourse of cyberculture. As Rosalind Krauss argues, the grid stands for a 'kind of originary purity'; it appears as the constant, impervious structure which undergirds and orders the multiple layers of representation which surround it.[15] The other favoured term for the microelectronic network – the 'matrix' – has its own 'originary' connotations, as Claudia Springer points out, being derived from the Latin mater, meaning both mother and womb.[16]

If we are to attend to cyberculture's covert yearning for the primal truth of nature, then we should also recognise ecology's furtive desire to witness change, transformation, the irruption of the new. Against the impious velocities of the microelectronic era, Rifkin defends the enduring cycles and rhythms of the natural order. Yet, he is desirous of a universe '… teeming with life, a world spontaneous, unpredictable, dynamic, rhapsodising …'[17]: in short, a biotic realm imbued with much the same qualities that have excited both the modernist and the cybercultural imaginations. However much they might complain of information overload in the everyday world, contemporary nature lovers, no less than netsurfing cyberians, wish to immerse themselves in an endless stream of sensory stimulation which flows from an authentic source.

Both ecologists and cyberculturalists, then, wish to absorb themselves in alternative realities that are rich in meaning and stimuli. But neither wish to be constantly reminded of how they arrived there, or how this 'reality' is constructed and sustained. In the case of cyberculture, what often seems like an infatuation with technology might be better read as a fascination with the self-overcoming or disappearance of technology. Just as early cinema audiences were enraptured by the seemingly magical materialisation of moving images, so too is there a sense of excitement which surrounds the apparent receding of the interface in fully immersive computer simulations. 'As screens are dissolving', exclaims computer graphic artist Nicole Stenger, 'our future can only take on a luminous dimension.'[18] To enjoy all the benefits of a technology in this way without being aware of its presence is a recurrent desire, as philosopher Don Ihde has noted. As he summarises this position:

> I want the transformation that the technology allows, but I want it in such a way that I am basically unaware of its presence. I want it in such a way that it becomes me. Such a desire ... belongs equally to pro- and anti-technology interpretations of technology.[19]

The extended capacities of perception made possible by the latest technologies play a constitutive part in both the ecological and cybercultural visions, I will be arguing. In the first case, the longing for an immaculate materiality precludes any lasting recognition of the contribution of a succession of technological media to the construction of the particular 'nature' to which ecologists are now committed. In the second case, the ecstatic reception of the latest technologies as a sort of 'post-medium' delivering an immaculate immateriality tends to occlude their continuity with all prior modalities. In both senses, a real/unreal dichotomy is fortified. As Scott Bukatman puts it, updating Jean Baudrillard's pronouncement on Disneyland: 'Virtual reality is ... a simulation whose function is to make the real world seem more real.'[20] Conversely, we could say that pristine nature is a simulation which serves to make the other realities look less real.

Indeed, some cyber-theorists – old enough to have a foot in both camps – have found ways to play off dual realities against each other, to their mutual advantage. For Michael Heim, the benefit of spending time in the limitless, infinitely malleable realm of virtual reality is that it provides a counterpoint to that 'real, anchored world' which is characterised by biological finitude and 'a sense of rootedness in the earth'.[21] Similarly, Michael Benedikt contends that: 'Real reality – the air, the human body, nature, books, streets

... in all its exquisite design, history, quiddity, and meaningfulness may benefit from both our renewed appreciation and our no longer asking it to do what is better done "elsewhere".'[22] Or as Jaron Lanier puts it, virtual reality 'may help the ecology movement because it helps people appreciate nature in an intense way as a point of comparison'.[23]

But as they attend to this impossible task of shoring up the real, both ecology and cyberculture draw upon the resources of the inverse position, that of their shadow counterculture. Ecology, I want to suggest, increasingly avails itself of the latest technical modalities to promote 'the strong bond with untrammelled nature', more often than not unintentionally and unreflexively. On the other side of the coin, cyberculture forges ahead with new modes of simulation of 'reality', taking the fleshly world it so often disavows as a phantom referent for the new designer universe it introduces and celebrates.

Mediating Ecology, Greening Cyberspace

What the ecological project calls for is not more wildlife theme parks or computer simulations but the preservation or regeneration of entire ecosystems, or significant parts thereof. The primary aim is, within certain practical limits, 'to allow all entities (including humans) the freedom to unfold in their own ways unhindered by the various forms of human domination'.[24] While the ultimate value of 'thinking globally' is espoused, ecologists generally agree that the best place to start developing an ecological consciousness is in some local biotic community. As William Devall suggests: 'Total identification with "organic wholeness" is possible only after identification with some living being more immediate and tangible.'[25]

The concomitant of ecology's valorisation of the encounter with 'the real world' is a suspicion of images, a repudiation of the value of representation in general.[26] But in its contemporary manifestation, it would seem impossible to disentangle the doubled desire for intimacy and global awareness from the growing availability of images of 'nature'. On the one hand, our ability to imagine the world in its completeness or its globality, Susan Sontag has argued, is a condition of the 'photographic enterprise'.[27] On the other hand, the desire to see things closely – 'to get hold of an object at very close range' is also conditioned by the proliferation of 'mechanically reproduced' images, as Walter Benjamin first noted over half a century ago.[28] In this sense, the ecological ideal of an intimate, direct encounter with natural beings countermands the invisibility of the wild animal which was its normal condition prior to the era of photography.[29] Moving image has also played its part in the realisation of ecology's 'visionary' capacities, particularly through the genre of nature movies, which Disney Studios helped popularise in the 1950s and 1960s. These set new standards of visual expectation by revealing 'nature's mysteries' in close-up, slow motion, time-lapse exposure and 'living colour'.

Ecologists continue to rage against the machinery of nature's domination. Imagining itself to be in confrontation with the solid impervious forces of production, however, the movement finds itself more often in confluence with a pliant, accommodating stream of image-conveyed consumerism. In this milieu of prodigious visuality, environmentalists and ecologists are themselves drawn into graphical representation to impart their message. Taking as an example a successful advertising campaign to protect Tasmania's Franklin River, featuring a particularly 'sublime' wilderness image, Geoffrey Batchen points to the dilemma of ecological promotion. The ad, he contends, 'promises the possibility of a totally pristine environment, untouched by human hand, a promise paradoxically denied by the very existence of this photograph'.[30]

The ability to see or hear from afar requires a technological prosthesis: ecology wants the benefits of the artificially extended human sensorium, yet at the same time it wishes its object to remain inviolate. But immaculate perception and enhanced visionary capacities are an impossible combination. Matter and image have been brought into an integrated circuit, and the current will continue to flow. Not surprisingly, the Franklin River campaign precipitated an influx of tourists into the area resulting in a 'wilderness resource management' problem.[31] In promoting the cause of nature, a previously remote and obscure region has been opened up as a landscape of visual consumption. Ecology's twin injunctions to behold nature intimately and globally are perfectly in keeping with the logic of representation in the twentieth century, they are at one with the 'rituals of transparency' that are bringing every conceivable object, entity and event out of obscurity and into circulation.[32]

Matter and image, biophysicality and its representations have in fact been 'contaminating' each other for some time: perhaps for as long as human activity has been documenting itself. Few would deny the existence of a materiality that precedes our inscriptions – or what Katherine Hayles refers to succinctly as the 'unmediated flux'.[33] But the 'nature' we fantasise about, visit, inhabit and modify is inevitably a cultural production, an expression of our capacities for symbolically-mediated action. As Haraway proposes, this nature might best be seen as a co-construct, an artefact arising out of the interchange between humans and non-humans, both of which are construed as 'material semiotic actors' with their own needs, drives, objectives.[34] Ecology falls short of the notion of a co-production by privileging the non-human side of the equation; failing to recognise that human symbolic activity and its technological extensions not only destroy but also construct nature. Cyberculture, on the other hand, has a tendency to deny the part played by non-human entities – and our own corporeality – in the hewing of artifactual worlds from prior artifactual worlds and from the flux that precedes them.

In the earliest 'paradise' gardens, modelled after Edenic myth, the 'stuff' of biophysicality was wrought to the specifications of the oral or textual representation. This in turn would have had consequences for the perception of 'unwrought nature'. Later, in the 'picturesque' aesthetic of the early modern era, painters sought to reproduce select natural scenes with fidelity, whilst nature was in turn landscaped so that it might more closely resemble the painterly ideal: the two modes of representation colluding in the emergence of a new appreciation of open prospects and rugged contours. In our own century, the mass-mediated proliferation of photographic, cinematic and televisual images of nature has come to constitute an anticipation of 'reality' which is profound and all-pervasive in its effects.[35] Such is the aesthetic and technical virtuosity of this output, that the material world has come to appear most often as a pale shadow of its reproduced self; a process from which the ecological imperative cannot be exempted. As Russell Berman observes: 'any given piece of coastline, any single craggy peak cannot measure up to the standards set by the nature photographers and the Sierra Club calendars.'[36]

Increasingly, however, interpretations of the ecological vision are materialising in a form which renders 'nature' almost as accessible, as variated, and as enchanting as it is in its image-form. Drawing on the techniques of the theme park, simulated wildernesses are being constructed in zoos, museums, urban parks, resorts and even shopping malls. Often combining live fauna and 'animatronic' beasts, living flora and fibreglass 'evergreens', these assemblages offer immersive multisensory experiences of the sort of environments that are familiar from wildlife films and nature magazines. Invariably, 'the message that the real environment must be preserved' is an integral part of the scenario.[37] While such contrivances may be anathema to most radical ecologists, it can be argued that they provide tangible elements of the prescribed 'communion' with non-human lifeforms and landforms that many urban dwellers would otherwise forego, albeit in a kind of parodic inflation of ecology's intimacy/globality imperative.

But the scope of 'identification' with diverse entities is taken still further at many of these sites. Searing through the outer layers of simulacra are even more intense windows of simulation; the ensemble of video and computer screens which take the spectator closer to nature's most illustrious surfaces, deeper into its inner workings. In its quest to fulfil the promise of the Edenic myth, ecology has upped the ante, raised the expectations of its audience, amplified the desire for the solace of enchanted gardens. 'Ordinary' image-making and its redoublings into materiality are becoming inadequate to the task. A new regime of sensory effects begins to take shape in our midst: that of digitality and the electronic networks.

Because they are ultimately configured by electric pulses too small to be seen and calculations too rapid to be comprehended, and because they disavow any one-to-one relationship with a recognisable world, the products of digitality seem to issue from a universe of their own. 'Digital creations are not the offspring of any medium and have no home in physical reality', writes Timothy Binkley.[38] However, as computation has expanded to incorporate the representational functions of other media, so too has it inherited many of their themes, tropes and idioms. Digitally configured audio-visuality is now picking up where previous generations of simulacra leave off.

Ecologists have not been alone in their disinclination towards this latest mode of simulation. As Paul Brown recounts, critics and curators at the SIGGRAPH conference of 1989 were still delivering the verdict 'that computer art is cold, intimidating and heartless'.[39] Certainly, the first visualisation techniques – from the sine/cosine type display graphics on the monitors of the 1950s to the vector graphics of the 1960s' drawing systems – seemed to highlight the ratiocinative qualities of the computer.[40] Moreover, as early techniques for rendering objects in 3-D relied upon the arrangement of simple polygonic forms, they were much more suited to the depiction of hard-edged machined objects than the more irregular and organic forms of the biophysical world. This meant that when nature was modelled, it tended to look as though it had been reduced and standardised to industrial specifications.

But this was a transitional phase. Computer science and computer art have since colluded in the development of a range of techniques which result in more 'lifelike' effects, from the utilisation of fractal geometry, to provide the appearance of complexity – to the mapping-on of texture and pattern. In this way, digital creations have now attained the level of minute and circumstantial detail that has previously distinguished the contrived image from the captured. This comes through in an account of the computer graphic artistry required in the animated digital sequences of *Jurassic Park* (1993). As one of the artists recounts: '... We had to create the appearance of living, breathing dinosaur skin. We came up with texture maps for all the surface detail – the reptilian bumps, the sheen, water lines, dirt, little shiny spots from where they rub on trees, wet eyes, yellow teeth.'[41]

Given the continuity with more established media, it is not surprising that the prime goal of digital graphics has been the achievement of 'photorealism', in other words, the kind of idealised imagery we have come to expect from conventional photography and cinematography. While the cinematographic uptake of computer simulation amply demonstrates its mimetic capabilities, however, it precludes one of the fundamental attributes of the computer–human interface: the capacity for interactivity. Video games give a better impression of interactive possibilities, as do the more open-ended 'God-games' like 'SimEarth' or 'SimLife', in which a player takes control of a range of variables and seeks to direct and sustain the workings of a complex proactive 'ecosystem'. As McKenzie Wark notes, a game like 'SimEarth' abstracts from global ecological conditions, but by doing so with a strong interactive dimension, it involves the player personally in events which would otherwise seem remote and incomprehensible.[42] The Aquazone 'virtual aquarium' demonstrates that interactivity is acceding to photorealistic standards. Pet lovers get to breed their own digital goldfish, which then grow, swim and reproduce amidst a richly detailed marine environment. If the cyber-fish are not regularly fed, have their water cleaned and parasites kept under control, they are likely to go 'belly-up' in a rather convincing fashion. As the sales manager of the product relates: 'We had a couple who phoned us in tears when their fish died.'[43] This we might take as a vindication of Rifkin's or Roszak's fears of the reduced and simplified computer model being mistaken for the real thing. Alternatively, we might read it as evidence that digital imagery is attaining the very levels of detail, dynamism and sensuousness which these theorists could not countenance in the cybernetic sphere.

The point I wish to underscore here is that the dreams of ecology and the fantasies of cyberculture share the same cultural field and should be seen as being mutually implicated in the generation of the latest wave of simulacra. Ecology constantly challenges representation to find novel ways of bridging the gulf between subject and nature. In a fallen world, the unintended consequence of the quest for the enchanted garden is that it drives simulation to ever new heights: unconsciously, ecological reveries ascend into the ether of cyberspace. On the other hand, the products of digitality – the insecure offspring of pure abstraction – desire a home, a place in the material world. Lurking just beneath the surface of cyberculture's renunciation of matter is a desire to put down roots, to connect with the 'natural substrate' – which is to say, to touch base with all the preceding layers of representations. So digital simulation nominates photorealism or 'naturalism' as its ideal, it takes the perfect reproduction of nature as the measure of its achievement, the evidence of its belonging to the world. Unknowingly – because each is blind to the other in itself – ecology and cyberculture conspire in the production of ever more elaborate artifactual natures.

Wild Life: In Silico and In Vivo

The potential for a seamless interchange with nature takes a further step with the much hyped development of the 'virtual reality' interface – which offers the illusion of full immersion in a data environment through the use of wrap-around binocular screens, tracking devices and near instantaneous or 'real-time' image adjustment. Again, in both achieved and imagined virtual spaces, the simulation of nature is a central theme. An early example was the demonstration model designed by the Human Interface Laboratories of Seattle:

> Octopus's Garden was an undersea plateau with large rock formations, swaying seaweed, and a school of fish that drifted in and out of sight. The large pink octopus moved about under the control of the system operator using the mouse ... One could jack into ... the perspective of the octopus, school of fish, or starfish.[44]

Pondering the potentialities of the digital modelling, Sherman and Judkins muse that 'in a strange sort of way, virtual reality has more realness than real reality'.[45] By this, they refer to the nascent capacity to render any object into any form, at any scale: thus opening up bringing previously inaccessible regions to human sensory experience. With the development of gloves, and ultimately full-body suits which can transmit a sense of pressure or resistance to the body beneath, the VR environment will be endowed with haptic qualities, adding a further dimension to the illusion of physical presence. Commentators have imagined numerous applications for the rendering of objects into tactile, navigable environments; from the inside of a cell to an anthill to a galaxy. 'They could be models of molecules ... and you could move about within these molecules with your whole body to examine their structures.'[46] Moreover, such environments might well be animated, endowed with an apparent 'life' of their own. Nicholas Negroponte, for example, anticipates the construction of a virtual *Jurassic Park*, populated by dinosaurs with 'appearance, personality, behaviour and purpose'.[47]

In such a scenario, the simulated natural being and the participating subject would be effectively 'communicating' in real time through their mutual integration into a common loop of feedback effects. The immediacy of this 'conversation' is made possible by the fact that all the participating bodies are entirely digitised, which means that information regarding the various gestures and movements is being shuttled back and forth at close to light speed. But we should not let this extreme case overshadow the fact that throughout the broader cultural field, the circuits connecting images and objects, images and events, images and other images, are everywhere becoming tighter and faster. Electronic networks now pervade our entire socio-cultural milieu, being both indicative and constitutive of our present obsession with communication, information exchange, feedback.

Ecology, I have been suggesting, is not immured from the prevailing techno-cultural condition. In the current climate, it is no longer enough that natural beings are seen or encountered, henceforth contact must be extended into an ongoing dialogue. Once we were content with recorded 'whale song', now as deep ecologist Bill Devall relates, we must converse:

> Recognising that our connections with other mammals can be expressed in music, Jim Nollman and an organisation called Interspecies Communication began playing music to orcas in the bays and estuaries off Vancouver Island. In a recording of these encounters, the orcas are heard responding by vocalising in time to the music.[48]

The San Diego Zoo now conceives of its animals as 'mediums of communication' with its visitors;[49] conservationist Michael Fox backs his condemnation of animal captivity by recounting that 'he had tried during a visit to the National Zoo to look into the animals' eyes and they did not look back'.[50] Either way, there is an assumption of the normality of an exchange of information across species boundaries: another version of the dreams of unimpeded message-flow and 'universal translation' that permeate cyberculture.

Not surprisingly, the digital metamedium can contribute to the process of interspecies communication. The Interactive Plant Growing Project, designed by digital artists Christa Sommerer and Laurent Mignonneau, involves a selection of living plants and a large monitor displaying an animated digital graphic garden. Each of the live plants has receptors in its roots, which are wired to the artificial plant program. As visitors move around and interact with the living flora, the electrical tension between human and plant is transmitted to the simulated garden, where it impacts upon the visuals, causing new virtual plants to sprout, changing growth rates, colour and leaf orientation. As Sommerer recounts: 'People are astonished that the plants can sense something, without even being touched. People change when they see that a plant is a living organism that should be respected.'[51]

Cybernetic culture's tendency to hyperbolise the initiatives of ecology is extended in its latest take on the notion of identification with nature. When pioneer ecologist Aldo Leopold used the phrase 'thinking like a mountain' – often cited by subsequent ecological thinkers – to evoke the experience of overcoming a human-centred perspective and identifying with a wider natural community, he was speaking metaphorically.[52] Cyberculture, on its ascent up the asymptote to pure presence and total transparency, takes this injunction literally. As we have seen, three-dimensional modelling in the computer permits the viewer's perspective to be changed with relative ease, which raises the possibility of negotiating a synthetic environment from the point of view of another organism, as in the case of the Octopus's Garden. The corporeal projection of fully-immersive virtual reality permits a certain malleability of bodily form, with regard to size, type of motility, and configuration of the sensory organs. As Jaron Lanier reports from the Virtual Programming Languages Research Laboratories: 'We've found that people are very good at learning to use other virtual bodies, like a lobster or a gazelle. It's as if your brain doesn't care what body you have so long as it has enough feedback.'[53] The improvisable nature of embodiment and perception does not stop with the animal world. 'In theory, anything can be experienced', Sherman and Judkins propose: 'Be a zinc sulphate molecule in a reaction, a plant in a drought or even a snowflake.'[54]

Whatever the level of 'naturalism' which these other beings or bodies attain, they remain our own creations, another version of nature tuned to the measure of our fantasies and expectations. For all the supposedly infinite possibilities of cyberspace, there is a sense in which most of its contents – attained or imagined – have an air of familiarity about them. Despite its construction as the latest frontier, or the new wilderness, cyberspace is still largely a container for the pre-digested, for the always already represented: which is to say, it lacks the otherness with which nature is still endowed (when it evades total visibility and enforced communication). As Jean Baudrillard puts it: 'The screen works much like a mirror … (it) transforms the process of relating into a process of commutation into the One and the Same.'[55] In his view, there is little to get excited about in the current rage for communication, for all this promises is more of the same, only faster. 'By definition, communication simply brings about a relationship between things already in existence. It doesn't make things appear.'[56]

For the ecologically-minded, the fascination with the biophysical realm lies not only in its givenness, but in its 'autopoietic' quality – its capacity for self-creation, its inherent propensity to 'make things appear'. As I suggested earlier, ecologists have not been immune to the modernist desire for spontaneity, novelty, dynamism: they just seek it where others tend to see stasis. Ecological texts abound with ardour for the wildlife which populates the planet, for as-yet undiscovered species or systems, and, not the least, for the forms and structures which might yet evolve, if ecosystems are allowed to maintain their integrity. The horror of overdevelopment abides not only in the fact that it makes things disappear, but also in its attenuation of natural evolutionary potential – the loss of possibility for new things to appear.

This desire for autopoeisis now enters the cybernetic arena. Recently, there has been a burgeoning of interest in the construction of digital entities which exhibit their own capacity for reproduction, self-creation and autonomous behaviour. The experiments being conducted in the new field of 'artificial life' – a subdiscipline of biology – have captured the cybercultural imagination, and may even intimate a reconceptualisation of the computer, from a medium of processing, representing and communicating, to an environment in which new things come to be. 'A-life' researchers work with virus-like strings of code, only instead of releasing these into the networks, they set them to interact in a contained section of computer processing space. As Manuel De Landa puts it: 'The exercise will be considered successful if novel properties, unimagined by the designer, emerge spontaneously.'[57]

A state of the art a-life 'ecosystem' may be made up of several varieties of organisms, each of which is comprised of a set of 'genes' or digitised instructions. These instructions determine the initial behavioural patterns of each creature, as well as its visual appearance on the screen. The organisms have some form of sensory input, such as an ability to recognise neighbouring organisms, and are able to 'mate' by meeting and exchanging chromosomal instructions with certain other specimens. This transmission process, which may include an element of mutation, allows for the generation and selection of novel forms. The more successful creatures survive and interbreed, new adaptive structures and behaviours may evolve, and mutations occur and are selected for or against. In Thomas Ray's Tierra program, for example, some creatures quickly developed 'parasitic' traits, 'hosts' soon responded by adopting 'immunising' strategies; these were highly effective until higher level cooperative 'hyper-parasites' evolved.[58]

Hoping to evolve far more complex organisms, Ray's latest proposal is to use the spare processing space of terminals linked by the global networks. With appropriate safeguards to protect existing files, he hopes to use the resources of this expansive environment to trigger off the 'Big Bang of complex digi-biotic diversity'.[59] Either by way of Ray's 'global wilderness reserve for computer viruses', or by the more illicit and haphazard viral infections of the Net, journalist Julian Dibbell raises the possibility that an entire ecology of interacting digital entities 'might someday flourish in the midst of our daily routines, unplanned, uncontained, ill-comprehended, and irrepressible'.[60] And we might also expect that many of these 'organisms' will be brought out of the hidden interstices of the central processing units and into the light of graphic visualisation. Whilst today's a-life organisms generally manifest themselves on the screen as little more than shifting configurations of colour-coded flecks or blocks, the convergence of scientific techniques with aesthetically-driven procedures is already engendering a range of more visually appealing virtual entities. A-life researcher Peter Oppenheimer proposes that: 'If we keep an open mind and a heightened awareness, then the menagerie of artificial life-forms that we create will be rich, meaningful and beautiful.'[61]

The 'future', then, may not be as 'programmed in advance' as Rifkin feared, but as vital, spontaneous and indeterminate as ecologists imagine nature to be. Henceforth we will be able to immerse ourselves in the processes of evolution, adaptation and speciation and all the other manifestations of natural dynamism about which ecologists have only been able to fantasise. Entities are being granted 'the freedom to unfold in their own ways unhindered by the various forms of human domination', and it could be happening in the immediacy, the pure presence of our domestic terminals. And as ecology goes to the ether, cyberculture looks set to finally attain its groundedness, to become a substrate of its own, a truly life-giving matrix. In the words of Christopher Langton:

> The ultimate goal of the study of artificial life would be to create 'life' in some other medium, ideally a virtual medium, where the essence of life has been abstracted from the details of its implementation in any particular model. We would like to build models that are so lifelike that they cease to become models of life and become examples of life itself.[62]

The Terrain of the Familiar

It will probably remain open to debate as to whether life can exist *in silico* as well as *in vivo*. There are currently no universally accepted criteria as to what defines life, and they are unlikely to materialise. What may be more important is to recognise that artificial life, like other cyber-natures, stands at the confluence of two mythic tributaries: an older one which dreams of an immaculate materiality and a much younger one which dreams of an immaculate immateriality. Both sets of fantasies seem to offer escape routes from the complexities and uncertainties of contemporary socio-cultural life, a condition which finds its paradigmatic expression

in the decentred 'hyperspace' of the urban landscape.[63] In relation
to the dense, seemingly indecryptable layers of signifying surfaces
and functional demarcations which comprise the late modern city
– an urbanism only slightly 'fictionalised' in the descriptions of Chiba
City or the Sprawl in William Gibson's cyberpunk novels[64] or in
Blade Runner's Los Angeles – both the natural wilderness and
cyberspace seem to be endowed with a kind of transparency, an
integrity, a purity of form.

The problematic delineation of nature itself takes its place
amongst the numerous blurred genres, categories and zonings of
the latter twentieth century. Even before the upsurge of cybernetics,
with its novel interpolations of body and electronic machinery, the
boundary between nature and culture was being irreversibly
compromised by new geographical interspersions of the built and
the biophysical. Ever since the diffusion of automotive travel and
cinematically-conditioned patterns of visuality, nature has been
increasingly subjected to reconstruction and relocation as an object
of visual consumption. Disney's placement of the lushly jungled
Adventureland just across the street from the aggressively futuristic
Tomorrowland was as much a distillation of spatial trends already
pervasive along the roadsides of post-cinematic America, as it was
a revolution in landscape design. From the eye-catching verdure
of roadside attractions, to the resort development and enhancement
of 'natural' sites, from the garden-filled atria of corporate buildings
and shopping malls to the latest urban wilderness simulacra, 'nature'
and the modern built environment have become progressively
interwoven.

Neither the implantation of cybernetic spaces nor the
identification and reclamation of areas of natural wilderness offer
viable alternatives to the complex spatiality of the contemporary
artifactual environment. Far from constituting 'other' worlds, these
developments add further layerings, facets and focal points to the
dense accretion of simulacra that comprises the terrain of the
everyday. Just as the boundaries of 'nature' have been rendered
ever more permeable by the uptake of the biophysical into new
forms and permutations, so too are we beginning to see the erosion
of the idea of 'cyberspace' as a distinct, self-contained sphere.
What already seems to be happening is that cybernetic functions
are dissipating through our quotidian spaces: screens, receptors
and conduits already abound, everyday devices, objects, even
materials are being implanted with cybernetic components, and
new forms of holography are now enabling digital graphic effects
to be projected into ordinary environments.[65] In short, the hype
surrounding totally immersive, virtual realities may have served as
a decoy, detracting attention from the more prosaic modes of

cyberneticisation, in a similar sense that the initially hard-edged countenance of digital graphics belied their capacity to represent nature.

Whilst the materiality of 'nature' and its more mobile representations have been mutually implicated for thousands of years, it is undeniable that the circuits linking matter and image, biophysicality and its simulacra, are becoming faster, tighter, more intensive and extensive. In this sense, Rifkin's fears that the radical mutability of form in digital constructs might pave the way for recombinant genetics and other modes of manipulating the structures of organic forms seem well founded. Relinquishing the notion of self-contained spheres, it is to be expected that 'novel properties, unimagined by the designer' might soon be irrupting across the material-semiotic continuum, which is certainly a cause for concern – as well as fascination. But to counter such developments by recourse to mythic formations of purity and absoluteness, I have been suggesting, is ultimately counter-productive, for these are the very impulses which fuel the processes of artifactualisation.

In forsaking the impossible ideals of pure nature or perfect artifice, we also foreclose on any universal or immutable standard by which to evaluate our particular interventions or co-productions. With neither nature nor cyberspace providing a 'tower beyond the reach of tragedy'[66] – a domain which transcends the fortuities of history or culture – we are propelled back into the impure and compromised domain of everyday socio-cultural life. In lieu of ecology's ethic of 'nature knows best' and cyberculture's principle of 'consensual hallucination' or instant redesignability, the contingent processes of cultural interpretation and social negotiation reassert themselves. As Katherine Hayles suggests, with regard to the construction of nature there is a need to consider the specificity of time and place, and the interests of positioned (which is not to say immobile) actors – both human and non-human.[67] It is also important to relate these particularities to the broad flow of historically-conditioned modalities of technological mediation, which have now attained a global significance. And not least, we should remain attentive to the twin desires for ethereal mutability and earthly foundations, neither of which shows any readiness to vanish from the historical stage.

Notes

1. Anne Chisholm, *Philosophers of the Earth: Conversations with Ecologists*, (London, Sidgwick and Jackson, 1972), p. xi.

2. Mark Dery, 'Flame Wars', (Special Issue: 'Flame Wars: the Discourse of Cyberculture'), *South Atlantic Quarterly*, 92 (4), Fall 1993, pp. 559–68: see p. 566.

3. Douglas Rushkoff, *Cyberia: Life in the Trenches of Hyperspace*, (San Francisco, Harper SanFrancisco, 1994), p. 205.

4. Cited in Vivian Sobchack, 'New Age Mutant Ninja Hackers: Reading *Mondo 2000*', (Special Issue: 'Flame Wars: the Discourse of Cyberculture'), *South Atlantic Quarterly*, 92 (4), Fall 1993, pp. 569–584: see p. 572.

5. Christopher Langton, 'Life at the Edge of Chaos', in Christopher G. Langton, Charles Taylor, J. Doyne Farmer and Steen Rasmussen (eds), *Artificial Life II: Proceedings of the Workshop on Artificial Life Held February, 1990 in Santa Fe, New Mexico*, (Redwood City, CA, Addison Wesley, 1992), p. 84.

6. John Davy, cited in Jeremy Rifkin, *Time Wars*, (New York, Henry Holt, 1987), p. 25.

7. Theodore Roszak, *The Cult of Information: The Folklore of Computers and the True Art of Thinking*, (London, Paladin, 1988), p. 247.

8. *Ibid.* p. 170.

9. Donna Haraway, *Simians, Cyborgs and Women: The Reinvention of Nature*, (New York, Routledge, 1991), pp. 149–81.

10. Max Oelschlaeger, *The Idea of Wilderness: From Prehistory to the Age of Ecology*, (New Haven, Yale University Press, 1991), p. 28.

11. Rushkoff, *Cyberia: Life in the Trenches of Hyperspace*, p. 204.

12. Warwick Fox, 'Deep Ecology: A New Philosophy of our Time', *The Ecologist*, 14, (5–6), 1984, pp. 194–200: see p. 196.

13. Rushkoff, *Cyberia: Life in the Trenches of Hyperspace*, p. 5.

14. Jurgen Habermas, 'Modernity versus Postmodernity', *New German Critique*, 22(winter) 1983, pp. 3–14, see p. 5.

15. Rosalind Krauss, *The Originality of the Avant-Garde and Other Myths*, (Cambridge, Mass., MIT Press, 1986), pp. 158–62.

16. Claudia Springer, 'The Pleasure of the Interface', *Screen*, 32, (3), 1991, pp. 303–23, see p. 306.

17. Jeremy Rifkin, *Algeny*, (Harmondsworth, Penguin, 1984), p. 252.

18. Nicole Stenger, 'Mind is a Leaking Rainbow' in Michael Benedikt (ed.), *Cyberspace: First Steps*, (Cambridge, Mass., MIT Press, 1991), p. 58.

19. Don Ihde, *Technology and the Lifeworld: From Garden to Earth*, (Bloomington, Indiana University Press, 1990), p. 75. See also Sobchack, 'New Age Mutant Ninja Hackers: Reading *Mondo 2000*', pp. 577–8.

20. Scott Bukatman, *Terminal Identity: The Virtual Subject in Postmodern Science Fiction*, (Durham and London, Duke University Press, 1993), p. 194.

21. Michael Heim, 'The Metaphysics of Virtual Reality', in Sandra Helsel and Judith Roth (eds), *Virtual Reality: Theory, Practice, and Promise*, (Westport, Meckler, 1991), pp. 32–4.

22. Michael Benedikt, 'Introduction' in Michael Benedikt (ed.), *Cyberspace: First Steps*, (Cambridge, Mass., MIT Press, 1991), p. 4.

23. Cited in Timothy Druckrey, 'Revenge of the Nerds: An Interview with Jaron Lanier', *Afterimage*, May 1991, pp. 5–9, see p. 8.
24. Warwick Fox, 'The Meanings of "Deep Ecology"', *Island Magazine*, Autumn 1989, pp. 32–5, see p. 33.
25. William Devall, *Simple in Means, Rich in Ends: Practising Deep Ecology*, (London, Green Print, 1990), p. 46.
26. See Andrew Ross, *The Chicago Gangster Theory of Life: Nature's Debt to Society*, (London, Verso, 1994), p. 182.
27. Susan Sontag, *On Photography*, (New York, Farrar, Staus and Giroux, 1973), p. 3.
28. Walter Benjamin, *Illuminations*, (New York, Schocken Books, 1969), p. 223.
29 See John Berger, *About Looking*, (New York, Pantheon Books, 1980), p. 14.
30. Geoffrey Batchen, 'Terrible Prospects', in Annette Shiell and Ann Stephen (eds), *The Lie of the Land*, (Monash University, National Centre for Australian Studies, 1992), p. 48.
31. McKenzie Wark, 'Third Nature', *Cultural Studies*, 8(1), 1994, p. 123.
32. See Jean Baudrillard, *The Ecstasy of Communication*, (New York, Semiotexte, 1988), p. 34.
33. N. Katherine Hayles, 'Searching for Common Ground', in Michael Soule and Gary Lease (eds), *Reinventing Nature? Responses to Postmodern Deconstruction*, (Washington, DC, Island Press, 1995), p. 49.
34. Donna Haraway, 'The Promises of Monsters: A Regenerative Politics for Inappropriate/d Others', in Lawrence Grossberg, Cary Nelson and Paula Treichler (eds), *Cultural Studies*, (London, Routledge, 1992), pp. 297–8.
35. See Jean Baudrillard, *The Evil Demon of Images*, (University of Sydney, The Power Institute of Fine Arts, 1987), pp. 13 and 27.
36. Russell Berman, *Modern Culture and Critical Theory: Art, Politics, and the Legacy of the Frankfurt School*, (Wisconsin, University of Wisconsin Press, 1989), p. 89.
37. Bob Mullan and Garry Marvin, *Zoo Culture*, (London, Weidenfeld and Nicolson, 1987), p. 60.
38. Timothy Binkley, 'Camera Fantasia: Computed Visions of Virtual Realities', *Millennum Film Journal*, 21, Winter/Fall 1988/9, pp. 7–43, see p. 19.
39. Paul Brown, 'Metamedia and Cyberspace: Advanced Computers and the Future of Art', in Philip Hayward (ed.), *Culture, Technology and Creativity in the Late Twentieth Century*, (London, John Libbey, 1990), p. 236.
40. See Andy Darley, 'From Abstraction to Simulation: Notes on the History of Computer Imaging', in Philip Hayward (ed.), *Culture, Technology and Creativity in the Late Twentieth Century*, (London, John Libbey, 1990), pp. 42–4.
41. Mark Dippe, cited in Don Shay and Jody Duncan, *The Making of Jurassic Park*, (London, Boxtree, 1993), p. 130.
42. Wark, 'Third Nature', p. 127.

43. Takashi Mineyoshi cited in Kim Eastham, 'Artifishal Experience', *Wired*, July 1994, p. 122.
44. Meredith Bricken, 'Virtual Worlds: No Interface to Design', in Michael Benedikt (ed.), *Cyberspace: First Steps*, (Cambridge, Mass., MIT Press, 1991), p. 376.
45. Barrie Sherman and Phil Judkins, *Glimpses of Heaven, Visions of Hell: Virtual Reality and its Implications*, (London, Hodder and Stoughton, 1992), p. 127.
46. Randal Walser, cited in Therese Welter, 'The Artificial Tourist', *Industry Week*, 1 October 1990, p. 66. See also Rushkoff, *Cyberia: Life in the Trenches of Hyperspace*, p. 43.
47. Nicholas Negroponte, *Being Digital*, (Rydalmere, NSW, Hodder and Stoughton, 1995), p. 119.
48. Devall, *Simple in Means, Rich in Ends*, p. 73.
49. Mullan and Marvin, *Zoo Culture*, p. 130.
50. Cited in Jon Luomo, *The Role of Zoos in Wildlife Conservation*, (Boston, Houghton, Mifflin, 1987), p. 188.
51. Cited in Mark Frauenfelder, 'The Interactive Life of Plants', *Wired*, 2.07, p. 35.
52. See Oelschlaeger, *The Idea of Wilderness*, p. 351.
53. Jaron Lanier cited in Paul Marks, 'VR: too much, too young?', *International Broadcasting*, August 1992, p. 50.
54. Sherman and Judkins, *Glimpses of Heaven, Visions of Hell*, p. 89.
55. Jean Baudrillard, *The Transparency of Evil: Essays on Extreme Phenomena*, (London, Verso, 1993), p. 54.
56. Jean Baudrillard, *The Revenge of the Crystal*, (London, Pluto Press, 1990), p. 24.
57. Manuel De Landa, 'Virtual Environments and the Emergence of Synthetic Reason', in (Special Issue: 'Flame Wars: the Discourse of Cyberculture'), *South Atlantic Quarterly*, 92, (4), Fall 1993, pp. 793–815, see p. 800.
58. See Steven Levy, *Artificial Life: The Quest for a New Creation*, (London, Penguin, 1992), pp. 218–28.
59. Julian Dibbell, 'Viruses are Good for You', *Wired*, 3.02 February 1995, pp. 126–33, 172–80, see p. 178.
60. *Ibid.* p. 179.
61. Peter Oppenheimer, 'The Artificial Menagerie', in Christopher Langton (ed.), *Artificial Life: Santa Fe Institute Studies in the Sciences of Complexity*, (Reading, MA, Addison-Wesley, 1988), p. 273.
62. Cited in Levy, *Artificial Life: The Quest for a New Creation*, p. 85.
63. See Fredric Jameson, *Postmodernism, or, The Cultural Logic of Late Capitalism*, (London and New York, Verso, 1991), p. 38.
64. See William Gibson, *Neuromancer*, (London, Grafton, 1986).
65. See Negroponte, *Being Digitial*, pp. 120–5.
66. The phrase is from a poem by Robinson Jeffers, an important influence on deep ecology. For a critical discussion, see Jim Cheney, 'The Neo-Stoicism of Radical Environmentalism', *Environmental Ethics*, 11 (4), 1989, pp. 293–325.
67. Hayles, 'Searching for Common Ground'.

CHAPTER 6

Welcome to Cyberia
Notes on the Anthropology of
Cyberculture

Arturo Escobar

This chapter discusses types of cultural analyses that might be possible to advance today on the social nature, impact and use of new technologies; it is based on the belief that computer, information and biological technologies are bringing about fundamental transformations in the structure and meaning of modern society and culture. Not only does this transformation offer itself clearly to anthropological inquiry, it constitutes perhaps a privileged arena for advancing anthropology's project of understanding human societies from the vantage points of biology, language, history and culture.

As a new domain of anthropological practice, the study of cyberculture is particularly concerned with the cultural constructions and reconstructions on which the new technologies are based and which they, conversely, contribute to shaping. The point of departure of this inquiry is the belief that any technology represents a cultural invention, in the sense that technologies bring forth a world; they emerge out of particular cultural conditions and in turn help to create new social and cultural situations. Anthropologists might be particularly well prepared to understand these processes if they are receptive to the idea that science and technology are a crucial arena for the creation of culture in today's world. Anthropologists must venture into this world in order to renew their interest in the understanding and politics of cultural change and cultural diversity.

The Nature of Cyberculture

While any technology can be studied anthropologically from a variety of perspectives – the rituals it originates, the social relations it contributes to creating, the practices developed around them by various users, the values it fosters – 'cyberculture' refers very specifically to new technologies in two areas – artificial intelligence (particularly computer and information technologies) and biotechnology. It would be possible to separate out these two sets of technologies for analytical purposes, although it is no coincidence that they have achieved prominence simultaneously in recent years. While computer and information technologies are bringing about a regime of *technosociality*, a broad process of sociocultural construction set into motion in the wake of the new technologies, biotechnologies are giving rise to *biosociality*,[1] a new order for the production of life, nature and the body through biologically-based technological interventions. Both processes, biosociality and technosociality, form the basis for what is termed here the regime of cyberculture. They embody the realisation that we increasingly live and make ourselves in techno-biocultural environments structured indelibly by novel forms of science and technology.

Despite this novelty, however, cyberculture originates in a well-known social and cultural matrix, that of modernity, even if it orients itself towards the constitution of a new order – which we cannot yet fully conceptualise but must try to understand – through the transformation of the space of possibilities for communicating, working and being. Modernity, in this way, constitutes the 'background of understanding' – the taken-for-granted tradition and way of being out of which we interpret and act – that inevitably shapes the discourses and practices generated by and around the new technologies. This background has created an image of technology as a neutral tool for releasing nature's energy and augmenting human capacities to suit human purposes.[2] The background responsible for this unproblematic and utilitarian view of technology must be made explicit as part of the anthropological investigation of cyberculture. Revealing the principles and assumptions that underlie the modern understanding of technology is an important step towards providing contexts for reorienting the dominant tradition. Some see the ultimate purpose of this reorientation as that of contributing to the development of technologies and technoliterate practices that might be better suited to human use and human purposes than they are at present.[3]

What sorts of questions might this brief presentation of cyberculture suggest to anthropologists? Let us begin by thinking about the following overall enquiries.

(1) What are the *discourses and practices* that are generated around/by computers and biotechnology? What domains of human activity do these discourses and practices create? In what larger social networks of institutions, values, conventions, etc. are these domains situated? In what ways do our social and ethical practices change as the project of technoscience advances? More generally, what new forms of social construction of reality ('technoscapes'), and what new forms of negotiation of such construction(s), are

introduced by the new technologies? How do people engage technoscapes routinely, and what are the consequences of doing so in terms of the concomitant adoption of new ways of thinking and being?

(2) How can these practices and domains be *studied ethnographically* in various social, regional and ethnic settings? What established anthropological concepts and methods would be appropriate to the study of cyberculture? Which would have to be modified? How, for instance, will notions of community, fieldwork, the body, nature, visuality, the subject, identity, and writing itself be transformed by new technologies?

(3) What is the background of understanding in which the new technologies emerge? More specifically, *which modern practices* – in the domains of life, science and technology – shape the current understanding, design and modes of relating to technology? What continuities and ruptures do the new technologies exhibit in relation to the modern order? Moreover, what kinds of appropriations, resistances or innovations in relation to modern technologies (for instance, by minority cultures) are taking place which might represent different approaches to and understandings of technology?

(4) What is the *political economy of cyberculture*? In what ways, for instance, are the relations between First and Third World restructured in the light of the new technologies? What new local articulations, with forms of global capital based on high technology, are appearing? How do automation, intelligent machines and biotechnology transform the labour process, the capitalisation of nature, and the creation of value worldwide? If different groups of people (classes, women, minorities, ethnic groups, etc.) are differentially placed in new technological contexts, how can anthropologists theorise and explore this ordering of technocultural construction? Finally, what are the implications of this analysis for a cultural politics of science and technology?

Modernity and Cyberculture

Cyberculture is fostering a fresh reformulation of the question of modernity in ways that are not so mediated by literary and epistemological considerations, as was the case during the 1980s. Whether or not we have entered an era of postmodernity, or if we still exist within a modified modernity ('late', 'meta', or 'hyper' modernity, as some have proposed) is an open question that cannot be decided prior to the investigation into the present status of science and technology. To the extent that science and capital still function as organising principles of dominant social orders, some insist that we have not yet taken leave of the space of modernity, despite the unprecedented modes of operation developed by both of these principles in recent decades.[4] If, as Foucault[5] has argued, the modern period brought with it particular arrangements of life, labour and language – embodied in the multiplicity of practices through which life and society are produced, regulated, and articulated by scientific discourses – cyberculture continues to act on these three domains, although bringing about very different configurations.

Modernity has been characterised by various theoreticians,[6] such as Foucault, Habermas and Giddens, in terms of the continuous appropriation of taken-for-granted cultural backgrounds and practices by explicit mechanisms of knowledge and power. Many aspects of life, previously regulated by traditional norms – in domains such as health, education, work, the body, space and time, even morality and social norms – have been progressively appropriated by discourses of science and the accompanying forms of technical and administrative organisation. With modernity, mechanical models of physical and social life gave way to models centred on the production and maximisation of life itself, including the coupling of the body and machines in new ways, in factories, schools, hospitals and family homes. There thus began an intimate imbrication of processes of capital and knowledge for the simultaneous production of value and life.[7] Societies, economies and cultures were thus restructured by capital and scientific knowledge in an extremely efficient manner relative to previous regimes. The spread of the written word, the pre-eminence of the machine, the control of time and space, and the biological and biochemical revolutions of the past 100 years brought into place unprecedented biotechnical arrangements which today find new ways of expression in cybercultural regimes. Machines became, to borrow a telling phrase, 'the measure of men'.[8]

Science and technology – or, better, 'technoscience' – has been central to the modern order, even if the relationship between science, technology and culture has remained insufficiently theorised. Heidegger's treatment of technology as a paradigmatic practice of modernity remains exemplary in this regard. Science and technology, for Heidegger, are ways of bringing forth new realities, new manifestations of being, even if the revealing of being by technology is problematic. For Heidegger, modern science necessarily constructs ('enframes') nature as something to be appropriated, whose energy must be released for human purposes. This is 'the danger in the utmost sense', to the extent that enframing leads to destructive activities and, particularly, to the destruction of other, more fundamental ways of revealing the essence of being ('*poiesis*'), which Heidegger sees present in the arts and in certain Eastern philosophies. Yet technology for Heidegger has an

Loo

important ontological role to the extent that the world becomes present for us through technological links of various kinds. It is through technical practices that the social character of the world comes to light.[9] More recently, some philosophers have theorised further the preeminence of technical rationality as the primary mode of knowing and being, even prior to 'theoretical' knowledge and science themselves.[10]

It is precisely the priority accorded to science and theory over technical creativity that has led moderns to believe that they can describe nature and society according to laws. Rather than as the effect of technological practices, nature and society thus appear as objects with mechanisms, which has resulted in the instrumental attitude towards them. Cyberculture seems to deepen these trends, initiated by modern biopolitical technologies in the production of life-worlds. Yet the new regimes that are emerging around the production of life, labour and language in the wake of artificial intelligence and biotechnology have a series of novel features which presage the advent of a new era, perhaps best visualised by contemporary science fiction. New science fiction landscapes are populated with cyborgs of all kinds (human beings and other organisms with innumerable prostheses and technological interfaces), moving in vast cyberspaces, virtual realities and computermediated environments.[11] But while science fiction writers and technology builders are extremely enthusiastic about, and generally uncritical, of these trends, it remains to be seen to what extent and in what concrete ways the transformations envisioned by them are in the process of becoming real. This is another task for the anthropology of cyberculture.'[12]

Look at film

The Anthropological Project: (1) Theoretical Formulations

Interest in science and technology on the part of social/cultural anthropologists has been growing steadily in recent years, linked to the broader and growing field of science and technology studies (STS). STS topics of interest to anthropologists in recent years have ranged from ethnographies of scientists, laboratory studies, and studies of reproductive and medical technologies, gender and science, ethics and values, and science and engineering education, to the more fashionable studies of new computer and biological technologies, virtual reality, virtual communities and cyberspace. An ongoing effort to theorise the anthropology of science and technology is also under way and promises to become an increasingly active and visible trend within the discipline of anthropology in the near future.[13]

Although the bulk of anthropological STS studies have taken place in highly industrialised countries, and while these studies have privileged the most recent technological innovations, this does not necessarily have to be the case. Indeed, given the centrality of Third World cultures and cultural diversity for anthropology, it is to be expected that STS activities will pay growing attention to STS issues in Third World contexts, without necessarily slowing down ethnographic research and theory construction in the 'First World'. It can even be argued that a partial shift of focus to the Third World is necessary, to the extent that the globalisation of cultural and economic production relies ever more on the new technologies of information and life. This is as true concerning biotechnology-driven development interventions in the Third World as it is regarding the cultural transformations effected by information technologies and the media. Whether it is in the domains of development, information or warfare,[14] the encounter between North and South continues to be heavily mediated and constructed by technologies of manifold kinds.

Recently, the impact of technologies such as television and video cassettes on local notions of development and modernity, and their effect on long-standing social and cultural practices, have been approached ethnographically.[15] From an earlier emphasis on worldwide homogenisation and generalised acculturation, the effect of cosmopolitan science and technology is now seen more in terms of their real or potential contribution to the formation of hybrid cultures and to processes of self-affirmation through selective and partially autonomous adoption of modern technologies.[16] This is particularly the case with microtechnologies, as opposed to large scale interventions such as industrial schemes and hydroelectric dams. However, as Hess convincingly argues, the effect of cosmopolitan technologies on Third World groups remains insufficiently understood, particularly from the vantage point of the cultural politics they set in motion, including issues of cultural destruction, hybridisation and homogenisation, as well as political economy and resistance. Work on these issues is advancing rapidly, particularly in connection with the redefinition of development.[17] The crucial question of the nature of cyberculture in/from the Third World, however, remains to be articulated.

Anthropological reflection on the relationship between culture and technology is of course not new. The impact of Western technologies on cultural change and evolution, for instance, has been a subject of study since the early 1950s.[18] Questions of technological control, political economy, macro/microtechnology distinctions have been broached. Nevertheless, studies of material culture and technology have suffered from dependence on what a reviewer of the field recently called 'the standard view of technology' (based on the assumption that 'necessity is the mother of invention', the decontextualisation of technology, and a telelogical vision that goes from simple tools to complex machines). Only with modern STS has the possibility arisen to see science and technology in relation to complex socio-technical systems; this 'lays the foundation once again for fruitful communication among social anthropologists, ethnoarchaeologists, archaeologists, and students of human evolution'.[19] It also fosters exchange between anthropologists and other disciplines involved in STS, such as philosophy, cognitive science and linguistics.

In the First World, attempts at articulating an anthropological strategy explicitly centred on new information, computer and biological technologies has just begun. An important precursor in this regard was Margaret Mead's work in the context of the emergence of cybernetics during the Second World War and up to the middle of the 1960s.[20] At the beginning of the 1990s, it is possible to identify three different proposals. The first proposal, by anthropologist David Thomas, builds on the growing literature on the notions of 'cyberspace'[21] and 'cyborg' – broadly speaking, a mixture of human and machine. Arguing that advanced forms of Western technology are bringing about a 'rite of passage' beween industrial and 'postorganic' societies, between 'organically human and cyberpsychically digital life-forms as reconfigured through computer software systems', Thomas calls on anthropologists to engage 'virtual worlds technologies during this early stage of speculation and development', particularly from the point of view of how these technologies are socially produced.[22] From print-based paradigms of visual literacy to the virtual worlds of digitalised information, this anthropologist argues, what we are witnessing is a transition to a new postorganic, postcorporeal stage that presents great promise in terms of creative social logics and sensorial regimes. As the locale for a new postorganic anthropology, cyberspace affords unprecedented possibilities for anthropologists in terms of realising the potential of this promise and combating the tendency to construct it as a space of purely economic contestations.

The second project, 'cyborg anthropology' – formally launched with a two-panel session held at the Annual Meeting of the American Anthropological Association (AAA) in San Francisco in December 1992, consciously takes as a point of departure the established activities of STS and the feminist studies of science and technology. While its overall domain of activity is the analysis of science and technology as cultural phenomena, the main goal of cyborg anthropology is to study ethnographically the boundaries between human and machines that are specific to late twentieth century societies. Believing that the adequacy of '*anthropos*' as the subject and object of anthropology – that is, the human-centred foundation of anthropological discourse, and the placing of agency solely on the skin-bound individual – must be displaced, the emerging cyborg anthropologists adamantly claim that human and social reality is as much a product of machines as of human activity, that we should grant agency to machines, and that the proper task for an anthropology of science and technology is to examine ethnographically how technology serves as agent of social and cultural production.[23]

Critical positions regarding these two projects are beginning to be articulated, most notably from the field of visual anthropology. Given the importance of vision for virtual reality, computer networks, graphics and interfaces, and for imaging technologies – from satellite surveillance, warfare and space exploration to medical technologies such as tomography and the visualisation of the foetus[24] – it is not surprising that the branch of anthropology most attuned to the analysis of visuality as cultural and epistemological regime, namely, visual anthropology, has been the first to react to both uncritical celebration of cyberspatial technologies (see Benedikt and Rheingold) and to anthropological projects centred on these latter. Claims by cyberspace designers that the new technologies will 'make the body obsolete, destroy subjectivity, create new worlds and universes, change the economic and political future of humanity, and even lead to a posthuman order', are in the best of cases, for these critics, wishful thinking motivated by the seduction of virtual reality and like technologies, and in the worst misguided efforts at engineering social reality.[25]

Rather than suggesting that a whole new anthropological subdiscipline is needed, Gray and Driscoll prefer to speak of 'anthropology of, and in, cyberspace'. While granting a certain novelty to new technologies, these authors recommend that anthropologists study technologies in the cultural contexts from which they originate and in which they operate, including their continued links to the dominant values of rationality, instrumentality, profit and violence. It is no coincidence, they continue, that virtual reality – one of the recent developments at the heart of the cyberspatial movements – has been and is likely to continue to be circumscribed by military and economic interests and that, despite their much touted potential for liberatory and humanising purposes, the military and profit-oriented applications will undoubtedly remain dominant. One must then examine these technologies from the perspective of how they allow various groups of people to negotiate specific forms of power, authority, representation and knowledge.

'The anthropology of cyberculture', as understood in this proposal, similarly agrees with the fact that we can assume *a priori* neither the existence of a new era nor the need for a new branch of anthropology. Indeed, as in the case of most anthropological analyses of cultural production, the discipline is in principle well suited to what must start as a rather traditional ethnographic project: to describe, in the manner of an initial diagnosis, what is happening in terms of the emerging practices and cultural transformations associated with rising technoscientific developments. However, given that these developments are increasingly unprecedented sites of articulations of knowledge and power, it is also pertinent to raise the question of the theoretical adequacy of established concepts in the light of their historical and cultural specificity.

In what ways? Some theorise that what is happening is a blurring and implosion of categories at various levels, particularly those modern categories that have defined until recently the natural, the organic, the technical and the textual. New discourses of biology, for instance, do not conceptualise living beings in terms of hierarchically organised organisms, but according to the language of communications and systems analysis, that is, in terms of engineered communications systems, command-control networks, purposeful behaviour, and probabilistic outcomes. Pathology is the result of stress and communications breakdown, while the immune system is modelled as a battlefield. In sum, notions such as organism and individual, so dear to pre-Second World War science, are being de-naturalised as never before. The boundaries between nature and culture, between organism and machine, are ceaselessly redrawn according to complex historical factors in which discourses of science and technology play a decisive role.[26] 'Bodies', 'organisms' and 'communities' thus have to be retheorised as composed of elements that originate in three different domains: the *organic*, the *technical* (or technoeconomic), and the *textual* (or, broadly speaking, the cultural).

The boundaries between these three domains are quite permeable, producing always assemblages or mixtures of machine, body and text: while nature, bodies and organisms certainly have an *organic* basis, they are increasingly produced in conjunction with *machines*, and this production is always mediated by scientific *narratives* ('discourses' of biology, technology, and the like) and by culture in general. 'Cyberculture' must thus be understood as the overarching field of forces and meanings in which this complex production of life, labour and language takes place. For some,[27] while cyberculture can be seen as the imposition of a new grid of control on the planet, it also represents new possibilities for potent articulations between humans, nature and machines. The organic, these critics suggest, is not necessarily opposed to the technological. Yet it must also be emphasised that new knowledge and power configurations are narrowing down on life and labour, such as in the human genome project; indeed, the new genetics – linked as well to novel computer techniques, its promise most eagerly visualised in the image of the biochip – might prove to be the greatest force for reshaping society and life ever witnessed in history. Nature will be known and remade through technique; it will be literally built, in the same way that culture is, with the difference that this process will take place through the reconfiguration of social life by micro-practices originating in medicine, biology and biotechnology.[28] Beyond the possibilities of new forms of genetic determinism, the relationship between nature and culture will be radically reconceived. Molecular biology is creating the sense of a 'new malleability of nature'; this is easily seen in the discourse on genetic diseases.[29] The 'right to normal genes' might well become the battle cry of an army of health experts and reformers who will effect a deployment of modes of practices of biosocial transformation not witnessed since 'the birth of the clinic' two centuries before.[30]

Hence the importance of devoting increasing attention to the social and cultural relations of science and technology as central mechanisms for the production of life and culture in the twenty-first century. Capital, to be sure, will continue to play a crucial role in the reinvention of life and society. But the worldwide spread of value today does not take place so much through the direct extraction of surplus value from labour, nor through conventional industrialisation, but by further capitalising nature and society through scientific R&D, particularly in the areas of artificial intelligence and biotechnology. Even the human genome, as mentioned above, becomes an important area for capitalist restructuring and, so, for contestation. The reinvention of nature and culture currently under way – effected by/within webs of meaning and production that link science and capital – must thus be understood according to a political economy appropriate to the era of cyberculture.[31] So far anthropologists have been silent on these pressing issues. We need to begin in earnest the study of the social, economic and political practices being brought about by the project of technoscience and its associated enterprises and institutions, including biotechnology, cyberspatial realities, and in general all those sites in which the new technologies of life, language and labour are being articulated.

The Anthropological Project: (2) Ethnographic Domains

As stated before, the general questions to be raised by the anthropology of cyberculture include the following: what new forms of social construction of reality, and of negotiation of such constructions, are being created or modified? How are people socialised by their routine experience of constructed spaces created by new technologies? How do people relate to their technoworlds (machines, reinvented bodies and natures)? If people are differently placed in these constructed spaces (according to race, gender, class, geographical location, 'physical ability'), how is their experience of such spaces different? In what ways are these spaces interpreted? Contested (the hermeneutics of cyberculture)? Finally, and more important, would it be possible to produce ethnographic accounts of the multiplicity of practices linked to the new technologies in various social, regional and ethnic settings? How do these practices relate to broader social issues, such as the control of labour, the accumulation of capital, the organization of life-worlds, and the globalisation of cultural production? One can begin to think of these questions in terms of possible ethnographic domains and concrete research strategies. Some clues concerning these domains already exist in the embryonic research projects existing at present. As an initial approximation, to be refined as the research advances, one can distinguish the following domains of investigating.

(1) *The production and use of new technologies*. These would include anthropological research focused on scientists and experts in sites such as genetic research laboratories, high-technology corporations, and virtual reality design centres, on the one hand, and the users of these technologies, on the other. Ethnographies in this domain would generally follow in the footsteps of the handful of ethnographies of modern science and technology conducted to date;[32] STS theorising, particularly in relation to anthropology;[33] and feminist studies of science and technology,[34] although they will have to be resituated within the conceptual space of the anthropology of cyberculture. A handful of ethnographic studies are already under way in this regard.[35]

A salient aspect of research in this domain is the ethnographic study of the production of subjectivities that accompanies the new technologies. That the computer is 'an evocative object', a projective medium for the construction of a variety of private and public worlds, has been shown by Sherry Turkle.[36] As the computer culture spreads, Turkle shows in her foundational study in the anthropology of computer cultures, more and more people start to think of themselves in computer terms. This includes not only the use of the computer as a model for the human mind but for one's life as well (one 'programs' one's life, for example). Cyberculture is indeed creating a host of veritable 'technologies of the self'. Although some of these technologies rely on a view of self as machine, their cultural productivity can only be assessed ethnographically. Virtual worlds, in fact – such as the use of anonymous computer role-playing games, such as MUDs (Multi-user Dimension and/or Dungeon), as therapeutic media – can be used by people as a way to move out of the self and into the world of social interactions. In other words, these media can become instruments for reconstructing identities in interactive ways, and sources of knowledge about other cultures and the outside world, as Turkle's recent work indicates.[37]

(2) *The appearance of computer-mediated communities*, such as so-called virtual communities, and generally what one of the most creative computer environment designers has called 'the vibrant new villages of activity within the larger cultures of computing'.[38] Anthropological analysis in this area can be crucial not only for understanding what these new 'villages' and 'communities' are but, equally important, for imagining the kinds of communities that human groups can create with the help of emerging technologies. We can anticipate active discussion on proper methods to study these communities, including questions of online/offline fieldwork, boundaries of the group to be studied, interpretation, and ethics.

A variant of this line of research is what Laurel termed 'interface anthropology'.[39] The creation of human–computer interfaces has been treated narrowly as a problem of engineering design which attempts to match tasks to be performed with the tools at hand. Yet the key question of the distinct user populations for whom the technologies are intended ('what do the users want to do?') is often ignored or inferred from statistical information. But children, teachers, computer games designers and users, fiction writers, architects, community activists etc. (without even mentioning aspects of crosscultural design) all have different needs and approaches regarding this basic question. The same interface might not work for everybody, and local ways of doing things might evolve with or against existing environments. An 'interface anthropology' that addresses this lack would focus on user/context intersections, finding 'informants' to guide the critical (not merely utilitarian) exploration of diverse users and contexts. The issue of interface design is also important in the development of hypertext, to the extent that it is the virtual environment created by the hypertext that allows a 'matrix' of knowledgeable users to interact with each other.[40]

(3) *Studies of popular culture of science and technology*, including the effect of science and technology on the popular imagery and popular practices. What happens when technologies such as computers and virtual reality enter the mainstream social world? The rise of a 'technobabble' is only the tip of the iceberg of the changes that are taking place at this level.[41] For Argentinian cultural critic Beatriz Sarlo, the principal point in this regard is to examine the aesthetic and practical incorporation of technology into daily life.[42] This is accomplished by people in middle and popular sectors

in ways that while undeniably modern, differ significantly from those intended by scientists. At the level of the popular sectors, the technological imagery elicits a reorganisation of popular knowledge and the development of symbolic contents. This has to be taken into account in the study of 'technoliterate practices'.[43] Since the mid-1980s, ethnographic studies of popular culture,[44] so salient in contemporary cultural studies and of growing appeal to anthropologists, are grappling with some of these issues. The imbrication of cultural forms with social questions, however, does not have to be restricted to ethnographic studies; it can also be gleaned from literature and other popular productions, as the work of Sarlo, Seltzer and Jenkins demonstrates.[45]

(4) *The growth and qualitative development of human computermediated communication (HCMC)*, particularly from the perspective of the relationship between language, communication, social structures and cultural identity. While HCMC shares many features with other forms of mediated communication well studied by linguists and linguistic anthropologists, such as telephone and answering machine messages, it also differs in important respects. Human interaction through computers must thus be studied from the perspective of the transcultural/transituational principles and 'discourse strategies'[46] governing any type of human interaction, but also from the specificity of the communicative and linguistic practices that arise from the nature of the media involved. Perhaps four dimensions of the process of construction of HCMC communities stand out as particularly relevant in this regard:[47]

(a) the relationship between machines and social subjects as producers of discourse at the threshold of the birth of an international 'cyberliterate' society;

(b) the question of the creation, distribution and access to those 'authorised' or 'legitimate' HCMC codes and languages (parallel to Bourdieu's 'legitimate' standard language) whose mastery and manipulation grants particular groups of HCMC practitioners (élites?) symbolic authority and control over the circulation of cyberculture;

(c) the role of HCMC in establishing links, giving cohesion to, and creating continuities in the socio-interactional history of group members, side by side with telephone conversations, regular mail, or face-to-face interaction. This might include research on talk, interaction and technology in work and leisure contexts; and hypertext as a linguistic entity to be re-created or transformed through collaborative acts between one person and an original database, or among many users performing operations on a given text or texts;[48]

(d) the shaping and reshaping of social and cultural boundaries both between a given HCMC community and other social communities, and within HCMC communities.[49]

An underlying question in this domain is the hypothesised transition to a post-scriptual society being effected by information technologies. If writing and its associated logical modes of thought replaced orality and its associated situational ways of thinking, the information age would be similarly marking the abandonment of writing as the dominant intellectual technology. In the same way that writing incorporated orality, information would incorporate writing, but only after an important cultural mutation. Theoretical and hermeneutical knowledge – so closely linked to writing – would likewise enter into a period of decline or, at least, of reconversion to a secondary form. New ways of thinking would be instituted, characterised particularly by the operational qualities necessitated by information and computation. Time would no longer be circular (as in orality) nor linear (as with the historical societies of writing), but punctual. Punctual time and the acceleration of information would entail that knowledge will not be fixed as in writing; it will evolve, as with the concept of expert systems.[50] These momentous changes would signify profound anthropological transformations. For anthropology, so dependent on writing and hermeneutical interpretation, they pose particularly difficult questions.

(5) *The political economy of cyberculture*: anthropologists have paid close attention, particularly in recent decades, to the analysis of communities in the historical and global contexts in which they are situated.[51] Cyberculture presents new challenges for the continued articulation of an anthropological political economy. What has been variously called 'the silicon order', 'microchip capitalism' and 'the information economy' entails deep changes in capital accumulation, social relations, and divisions of labour at many levels. New questions arise, such as the following:

(a) What is the relationship between 'information' and 'capital'? Is it appropriate to postulate, as some do,[52] the existence of a 'mode of information' akin to a mode of production? How can we theorise the articulation between information, markets and cultural orders? Cybernetic machines are becoming the basis of a 'society of control',[53] and an entire cyberocracy, or 'rule by way of information',[54] is emerging. How can anthropologists and others best explore issues of class, freedom and domination, accommodation and resistance in relation to this information order?

(b) The appearance of a cyberocracy calls for *institutional ethnographies* to be conducted from the perspective of the political economy of information. What are the major institutional sites within which key informational categories and flows are created and put into circulation? What perspectives of the world do these categories and flows represent, and how do they enact mechanisms of ruling that depend on certain groups' relations to the mode of production of information? These ethnographies would move from sites of computer-mediated production of information to its reception and use, investigating at each level the cultural dynamics and politics that 'information' sets into motion.

(c) Like information, science and technology have become crucial to capitalism, to the extent that the creation of value today depends largely on scientific and technological developments. This is as clear in the case of biotechnology as it is with computers. Anthropologists have maintained that the transformation of nature and ecosystems by capital is mediated by the cultural practices of the specific societies in which such appropriation takes place.[55] But the concrete forms of appropriation of life and labour by capital through the use of contemporary science exhibits novel features, such as in the case of the human genome project. Another development is the ever tighter imbrication of academy and industry in the biotechnological field.[56] There is a new political economy of information and commodities in the making. How does this affect the practice of biological anthropology?

In the case of the Third World, the biophysical milieu (nature) is increasingly represented as a reservoir of capital, to be exploited mostly by biotechnology in the name of the efficient and rational use of the environment. Local communities and social movements are enticed to participate in these schemes as 'stewards' of natural and social capital. In this way, biotechnology assists capital in the semiotic conquest of territories and communities: communities (or their survivors) are acknowledged as rightful owners of 'the environment' only to the extent that they acquiesce to treat it (and themselves) as capital.[57] The whole issue of 'intellectual property rights' linked to Third World natural resources – such as the patenting by multinational corporations of seeds and plant varieties and substances derived from stocks used by Third World 'traditional' societies – is emerging as one of the most disturbing aspects of the ecological phase of capital.[58]

The 'biorevolution' will affect all aspects of development. As three prominent observers remark, 'New technical forms ... will significantly change the context within which technological change in the Third World is conceptualized and planned. We suggest that the cluster of emergent techniques generically called "biotechnology" will be to the Green Revolution what the Green Revolution was to traditional plant varieties and practices.'[59] Plant genetics, industrial tissue culture, and the use of genetically manipulated microorganisms represent pathbreaking technologies in the context of Third World development. Corporations have clearly understood it in this way and are already in the lead of R&D. As Buttle, Kenney and Kloppenburg warn in their analysis of patterns of corporate behaviour in this area, the prospects are 'ominous'. Even more, the new technologies will have the capacity to extend their reach to regions and circumstances prohibited to the Green Revolution. What are the implications of these developments for studies of material culture and biological anthropology? How will these branches of the discipline deal with the regime of biosociality and the biorevolution in development? What are the implications for social movements?

(d) Finally, the restructuring of the relations between rich and poor countries in the wake of cyberculture must be considered. As some argue, high technology is resulting in a 'new dependency' of technology-poor countries on the leaders in the innovation and production of computer, information, and biological technologies.[60] Third World countries, according to these authors, must negotiate this dependency through aggressive technological modernisation coupled with social reforms. From an anthropological perspective, this suggestion is problematic; it, indeed, amounts to the continuation of the post-Second World War policies of 'development' which have had for the most part deleterious effects on the economies and cultures of the Third World.[61] Like development, technologies are not culturally neutral.

Are there different possibilities for Third World societies, other ways of participating in the technocultural conversations and processes that are reshaping the world? How can, for instance, social movements in Asia, Africa and Latin America articulate policies that allow them to participate in cybercultures without fully submitting to the rules of the game? Will most social groups in the Third World be in the position to even know the possibilities afforded by new technologies? A more general question is whether Third World governments would be interested in constructing the technological imaginaries that will be required to accede to the new technologies from the perspective of more autonomous design. This is doubly important since, as Sutz believes, 'there will not be a genuine social transformation without transforming the relation between society and the technologies it incorporates'.[62] To start paying attention to the local technological innovation that always takes place in the Third World – even in the context of the new technologies – is a first step towards gaining a sense of 'technological self-esteem'. But, one must ask, is it possible to approach the new technologies with an understanding that transcends their role in 'economic development' and the like? Moreover, what does 'cyberculture' look like from the perspective of the Third World? What does it mean?

Of special importance in discussing these issues in the Third World is the role of women in the electronics industry worldwide, but particularly as cheap labour in Japanese, US and European factories located in the Third World. The development of cyberculture rests, in many ways, on the labour of young women in electronic enclaves in South-east Asia, Central America, and other parts of the Third World.[63] If the effects of economic adjustment policies under pressure from the International Monetary Fund have fallen heavier on poor women,[64] the same is true of the restructuring that usually accompanies other neo-liberal measures, such as the 'opening' of the economy to international markets and the setting up of factories in 'free trade zones'. There is every reason to believe that electronics will continue to be favoured in industrial schemes in the Third World, under the aegis of multinational corporations; and there is also every reason to believe that young women will continue to be seen as the 'ideal' labour force by these industries. The effects of this process on the dynamics of gender and culture are enormous, as studies of maquiladoras and sweatshops have shown, although these studies have just begun in the electronics sector. Feminist anthropology and political economy have a great deal to contribute to this fundamental aspect of the construction of cyberculture.

More generally, anthropologists need to study in depth the class, gender and race aspects of the development of cyberculture and challenges to it. This entails analysis of emerging scientific discourses and practices and the formation of technoscientific élites, on the one hand, and of the potential of individuals, groups and social movements to articulate parallel or alternative technologies, ways of knowing, and social relations of science and technology, on the other.[65] Anthropological studies of cybercultures can contribute to provide contexts in which there emerge possibilities for relating to technoculture that do not exacerbate the power imbalances in society.

Rethinking Technology? Anthropology and Complexity

As we discussed at the beginning of this chapter, science and technology have remained captive to the historical mode of the West, particularly to the discourses of modernity. A narrow-minded, instrumentalist and economistic posture has characterised our 'common sense' understanding of technology, while science has tended to adopt linear and reductionistic paradigms. We have also argued that, rather than being neutral instruments that merely allow or facilitate certain human endeavours, science and technology entail the production of life-worlds and the division of the social field in certain ways; in short, the creation of culture. It is clear that these two different approaches to science and technology are in opposition. Can the entrenched modern signification be reoriented or destabilised, so as to foster a different understanding of technology, more fluid and attuned to its sociocultural role? New developments in science during the past two decades suggest paths towards this reorientation. Although they can barely be hinted at here, these trends are likely to become important sources of dialogue and insight for those wishing to articulate a critical cultural politics of science and technology in the coming decades.

Much as the designers of the new technologies believe that they are changing the world, so do the groups of scientists working on the development of the 'science of complexity' have no doubt that they are at the threshold of a great scientific revolution. Instead of emphasising stability in nature and societies, they emphasise instabilities and fluctuations; in lieu of reversible linear processes ('the linearity trap'), they have substituted non-linearity and irreversibility at the heart of scientific inquiry. Similarly, 'conservative systems' (physical systems considered in isolation from their surroundings) have given place to 'self-organising' systems; static equilibrium to dynamic equilibrium and non-equilibrium; order to chaos; fixed elements and quantities to patterns and possibilities; prediction to explanation as the goal of science. The science of complexity has also replaced nineteenth-century physics with modern biology as a model; consequently, it studies physical phenomena as complex biological processes ('non-organic life'), and practises kinds of analysis that are based on the concrete and the heterogeneous, not on the abstract, the homogeneous and the general. While Cartesian epistemology and Newtonian science sought to model the Order of Things according to the (scientific) Law, the science of complexity – though still searching for a general law of pattern formation of all non-equilibrium systems in the universe – believes in a pluralistic view of the physical world, on webs rather than structures, connections and transgressions instead of neat boundaries isolating pristine systems.

According to the scientists, developments in thermodynamics and mathematics during the past 20 years (the thermodynamics of irreversible phenomena and the theory of dynamical systems) pushed scientists into recognising that the gap between the physicochemical and the biological worlds, between the 'simple' and the 'complex', and between 'order' and 'disorder' is not so sharp and large as it was thought. On the contrary, these developments make clear that non-organic matter shows properties that are remarkably close to those of life-forms, leading to the postulate that life is not a property of organic matter *per se*, but of the organisation of that matter, and hence to the idea of non-organic life.[66] In a similar vein, scientists began to pay attention to the fact that simple systems (such as a simple chemical reaction and a mechanical pendulum) can generate extremely complex behaviours, while, at the other end of the spectrum, extremely complex systems can give rise to simple and easily quantifiable phenomena. Realising that 'inert' matter can show complex lifelike behaviour, and that phenomena that were previously outside the purview of science because they could not be described by systems of linear equations were in fact central to the universe, led these groups of scientists to launch the theorisation of complexity as the crucial scientific research programme for the final decades of the twentieth century and for many decades to come.[67]

The popularity achieved by fractals and chaos theory (a relatively small subset of complexity) in the mid-1980s helped immensely to put these developments on the map for the larger public. Chaos became the signifier for many things, few of which perhaps had to do with the actual scientific work going on. This popularity, however, raises an important question recently taken up by a group of literary theorists – the extent to which science and culture intertwine in the production of popular imaginaries. Chaos theory, according to these authors, echoes and participates in other cultural currents, such as certain aspects of poststructuralist theory and postmodern culture. The birth of chaos and complexity is not independent from the same historical ferment which gave rise to 'the postmodern condition': a world that was becoming at once more chaotic and more totalised; small causes resulting in big effects in the economy and the social order; recognition of the importance of information and rapid expansion of information technologies. 'Chaos' – or, better, 'chaotics', as Hayles[68] proposes – must then be seen as a force that is negotiated at diverse sites within the culture, including science and poststructuralism. Contemporary literature reflects this postmodern condition, whether it is expressed in the terms of the human sciences or the sciences of complexity.[69]

Be that as it may, the science of complexity has already developed an impressive vocabularly and theoretical corpus.[70] At the heart of complexity is the idea of self-organising phenomena generated by complex systems under certain conditions. The idea of self-organisation is of course not restricted to complexity science. In biology, the work of Maturana, Varela and co-workers[71] has made self-organisation (the *autopoiesis* of the living) the cornerstone of their theoretical biology and epistemology. Foucault's elaboration of the nature of discursive formations can likewise be seen as a theory of the self-organising character of knowledge systems.[72] Perhaps the more thorough view of the pervasive character of self-organising processes is the work of Deleuze and Guattari.[73] Whether it is in the domains of inert matter (geology), the sciences, political economy, or the self, what these authors find at work are 'machinic' processes, stratifications and territorialisations that develop into the structures that are well known to us. Thus Foucault's archaeologies of modern structures – the relatively rigidified and sedimented systems of the clinic, the prison, the market, or what have you – can be seen as the result of the more general dynamics described by Deleuze and Guattari under rubrics such as 'machinic assemblages', 'rhizomics' and 'nomadology'.

It is clear that technology has been essential to the appearance and solidifying of modern structures. Modern structures belong with the line, boundary making, disciplinarity, unity, hierarchical control, and the fixity of power even at the micro-level. Fractals, chaos, complexity nomadology would perhaps dictate a different dynamics and arrangement of life – fluidity, multiplicity, plurality, connectedness, segmentarity, heterogeneity, resilience. Not 'science' but knowledge of the concrete and the local; not laws but knowledge of the problems and the self-organising dynamics of non-organic, organic and social phenomena. There is some awareness among the scientists working out complexity that they are reversing a centuries-old dualistic attitude of the West, the binary logic, the reductionist and utilitarian drive. Some have attempted a link with Eastern thought.[74] Despite these realisations, however, the scientists (unlike authors such as Foucault, Deleuze and Guattari) still place too much emphasis on order and general laws, and have perhaps too quickly jumped into the intellectual game of applying the ideas of complexity to social phenomena like economies, social orders, evolution, and the rise and fall of civilisations. Their tendency to produce overencompassing theories that would link the physical, biological, social and cultural worlds, without making explicit the immense epistemological processes and assumptions at stake in this endeavour, is indeed troubling.[75] Some critics have begun to see it as such, perhaps rightly so.[76]

Complexity, itself, needs to be anthropologised, in other words. Yet it might offer insights to anthropology. Anthropological questions have hardly been tackled within the science of complexity, with the exception of a reformulation in progress of the theory of evolution to account for the role of learning and self-organisation (in addition to natural selection) in evolution, and the articulation of a more complex concept of adaptation from this perspective. In fact, the Santa Fe Institute labels a good part of its work as the understanding of complex adaptive systems. Although there is some interest in cultural complexity, the question has not been broached to any significant degree. Anthropologists, it can be argued, have generally been attuned to the complex nature of life, and have resisted reducing it to magic formulae and laws. Nevertheless, since the nineteenth century to Malinowski, Boas, Benedikt, Levi-Strauss and Geertz, the tendency to reduce the manifold complexity of cultural reality into neat descriptions of institutions, patterns, structures or exemplars has not gone away. Only in recent years has this tendency been modified with the development of forms of analyses that emphasise partiality, after finally giving up any pretence at general laws and accounts from the heights of objectivity.

What kinds of questions can anthropologists pose in relation to the new science? Can this scientific trend – seemingly so different from conventional science, yet so clearly entrenched in scientific culture – contribute to reorient the prevailing understanding of technology? What would a new understanding of technology be like? What kinds of social experiences and techno-practices would it foster? Is it really possible to destabilise (destratify, deterritorialise) modern technosocial, politicoeconomic and biosocial systems, as Deleuze and Guattari would propose? Technology itself, of course, must begin to be seen as a self-organising system of sorts. The rapid development and avatars of the computer industry (why did it develop towards the personal computer when everything was geared up towards big centralised computers?) show this much. Yet the articulation of technological understandings and policies that contribute to people's autonomous lives and self-organising experiences are many years in the future, if they ever become possible. But, if we are to believe those working on new ways of understanding the universe and social life – whether in science or in the humanities – the possibility might be there for a 'nomadology' of technology.

Anthropology without Primitives?

Anthropology, it continues to be said,[77] is still enframed within the overall order of the modern and the savage, the civilised self and the uncivilised other. If anthropology is to 're-enter the real world' and 'work in the present',[78] it will necessarily have to deal with the steady march of cyberculture. Cyberculture, moreover, offers a chance for anthropology to renew itself without reaching again, as it was the case with the anthropology of this century, a premature closure around the figures of the other and the same.[79]

These questions, and cyberculture generally, concern what anthropology is about: the story of life, as it has been and is being lived today, at this very moment.

What is happening to life in the late twentieth century? What's coming for the next?

Notes

1. Paul Rabinow, 'Artificiality and enlightenment: from sociobiology to biosociality', in J. Crary and S. Kwinter (eds), *Incorporations*, (New York, Zone Books, 1992), pp. 234–52.

2. Martin Heidegger, *The Question Concerning Technology*, (New York, Harper and Row, 1977).

3. Terry Winograd and Fernando Flores, *Understanding Computers and Cognition*, (Norwood, NJ, Ablex Publishing Corporation, 1986).

4. Jonathan Crary and Sanford Kwinter (eds), *Incorporations*, (New York, Zone Books, 1992).

5. Michel Foucault, *The Order of Things*, (New York, Vintage Books, 1973).

6. *Ibid*; Jurgen Habermas, *The Philosophical Discourse of Modernity*, (Cambridge, MA, MIT Press 1987); Anthony Giddens, *The Consequences of Modernity*, (Stanford, CA, Stanford University Press, 1990).

7. See Michel Foucault, *The History of Sexuality. Volume I*, (New York, Vintage Books, 1980), pp. 135–59. See also Felix Guattari, 'Regimes pathways, subjects', in Crary and Kwinter (eds), *Incorporations*, pp. 16–35; Gilles Deleuze and Felix Guattari, *A Thousand Plateaus*, (Minneapolis, MA, The University of Minnesota Press, 1987).

8. Michael Adas, *Machines as the Measure of Men*, (Ithaca, NY, Cornell University Press, 1989).

9. Martin Heidegger, *Being and Time*, (New York, Harper and Row, 1962).

10. Manuel Medina and Jose Sanmartín, 'Filosoffia de la Tecnología, INVESCIT y el Programma TECNAS', *Anthropos*, No 94/95, 1989, pp. 4–7. With the exception of a few philosophers like Heidegger and Ortega y Gasset and, more recently, authors like Jaques Ellul, Mario Bunge, Lewis Mumford and Juan David Garcia Bacca, the philosophy of technology only took off as a field in the 1970s and 1980s. Important in this regard have been the creation of Carl Mitcham's Philosophy and Technology Studies Center in New York, (since moved to Pennsylvania State University), a similar group at the Universidad Politécnia de Valencia, (INVESCIT), and the Society for Philosophy and Technology in the United States.

11. An entire genre of science fiction, known as 'cyberpunk' has been on the rise since the publication of William Gibson's *Neuromancer* in 1984, now considered a 'classic' of cyberpunk and the official point of origin of the cyberspatial era. For an introduction to cyberpunk, see Larry McCaffery (ed.), *Storming the Reality Studio. A Casebook of Cyberpunk and Postmodern Fiction*, (Durham, NC, Duke University Press, 1991).

12. Marcy Darnovsky, Steven Epstein and Ara Wilson, 'Radical experiments: Social movements take on technoscience', *Socialist Review*, 21(2), 1991, pp. 31–3.

13. For a directory and bibliography of anthropological STS studies, see David Hess (ed.), *The Social/Cultural Anthropology of Science and Technology*, (Directory, 1992 edition). See also David Hess and Linda Layne (eds), *Knowledge and Society. Volume 9. The Anthropology of Science and Technology*, (Greenwich, CT, JAI Press, 1992); Bryan Pfaffenberger, 'The social anthropology of technology', *Annual Review of Anthropology*, 21, 1992, pp. 491–516; David Hakken, 'Has there been a computer revolution? An anthropological approach', *Journal of Computing and Society*, 7(1), no date, pp. 11–28.

14. Manuel de Landa, *War in the Age of Intelligent Machines*, (New York, Zone Books, 1991).

15. Lila Abu-Lughod, 'The romance of resistance', *American Ethnologist*, 17(1), 1990, pp. 401–55; Gudrun Dahl and Annika Rabo (eds), *Kam-ap or Take-off. Local Notions of Development*, (Stockholm, Stockholm Studies in Social Anthropology); Néstor García Canclini, *Culturas Hibrídas. Estrategias para Entrar y Salir de la Modernidad*, (Mexico, DF, Grijalbo, 1990).

16. The case of the Kayapo in the Amazon rainforest, who have become adept at using video cameras, aeroplanes, and revenues from gold mining in the articulation and execution of their struggle, is already becoming legendary. For an insightful discussion of this case, see David Hess, *Science and Technology in a Multicultural World*, (1993).

17. *Ibid*; Arturo Escobar, *Encountering Development: The Making and Un-Making of the Third World, 1945–1992*, (Princeton, NJ, Princeton University Press, 1994).

18. See for instance the studies of L. Sharp, (1952) and M. Godelier on the effect of the introduction of steel axes on Australian aborigines and the Baruya of Papua New Guinea, respectively; Maurice Godelier, '"Salt currency" and the circulation of commodities among the Baruya of New Guinea', in George Dalton (ed.), *Studies in Economic Anthropology*, (Washington, DC, American Anthropological Association, 1971). For an excellent discussion of earlier studies, see Hess, *Science and Technology in a Multicultural World*.

19. Pfaffenberger, 'The social anthropology of technology', p. 513.

20. Mead was an active participant in the famous Macy Conferences on Cybernetics, as well as a central figure at the founding of the American Society for Cybernetics. Margaret Mead, H.L. Teuber and Heinz von Foerster (eds), *Cybernetics*, 5 vols, (New York, Josiah Macy Jr Foundation, 1950–56); Margaret Mead, 'Cybernetics of cybernetics', in Heinz von Foerster (ed.), *Purposive Systems*, (New York, Spartan Books, 1968). The life of this illustrious 'cybernetics group', which included besides Mead people like Gregory Bateson, Heinz von Foerster, Norbert Wiener and Kurt Lewin, is chronicled in a recent book by Steve Heims, *The Cybernetics Group*, (Cambridge, MA, MIT Press, 1991).

21. The term 'cyberspace' was first coined by William Gibson in *Neuromancer*, (London, HarperCollins, 1984), formally introduced to intellectual, artistic and academic circles in M. Benedikt's collection,

Cyberspace: The First Steps, (Cambridge, MA, MIT Press, 1991) and refers to the growing networks and systems of computer-mediated environments. For introductions to the concept of cyberspace, see also Marcos Novak, 'Liquid architecture in cyberspace', in *Cyberspace*, pp. 225–54. Rheingold, *Virtual Reality*, and Allucquere Rosanne Stone, 'Virtual systems', in J. Crary and S. Kwinter (eds), *Incorporations*, (New York, Zone Books, 1992), pp. 608–25.

22. David Thomas, 'Old rituals for new space. Rites of passage and William Gibson's cultural model of cyberspace', in Benedikt (ed.), *Cyberspace*, pp. 31–48.

23. This description is mostly taken from the manifesto presented at the panel 'Cyborg Anthropology I: On the production of humanity and its boundaries', (Gary Downey, Joseph Dumit and Sarah Williams, 'Granting membership to the cyborg image', presented at the panel, 'Cyborg Anthropology II', 91st Annual Meeting of the American Anthropological Association, San Francisco, 2–6 December 1992).

24. Donna Haraway, *Symians, Cyborgs, and Women. The Reinvention of Nature*, (New York, Routledge, 1991); de Landa, *War in the Age of Intelligent Machines*; Lisa Cartwright and Brian Goldfarb, 'Radiography, cinematography, and the decline of the lens', in Crary and Kwinter (eds), *Incorporations*, pp. 190–201; and Barbara Duden, *The Woman Beneath the Skin*, (Cambridge, MA, Harvard University Press, 1990).

25. Chris Hables Gray and Mark Driscoll, 'What's real about virtual reality? Anthropology of, and in, cyberspace', *Visual Anthropology Review*, 8(2), 1992, pp. 39–49.

26. Haraway, *Symians, Cyborgs and Women*.

27. *Ibid*; Rabinow, 'Artificiality and enlightenment: from sociobiology to biosociality'.

28. Rabinow, 'Artificiality and enlightenment'.

29. Evelyn Fox Keller, 'Nature, nurture and the human genome project', in Daniel Kevles and Leroy Hood (eds), *The Code of Codes: Scientific and Social Issues in the Human Genome Project*, (Cambridge, MA, Harvard University Press, 1993), pp. 281–99.

30. Foucault, *The Order of Things*.

31. Arturo Escobar, 'From organism to cyborg: elements for a poststructuralist political economy of ecology and biology', *Futures*, (forthcoming).

32. Bruno Latour and Steven Woolgar, *Laboratory Life: The Social Construction of Scientific Facts*, (Princeton, NJ, Princeton University Press, 1979); Bruno Latour, *The Pasteurization of France*, (Cambridge, MA, Harvard University Press, 1988); Emily Martin, *The Woman in the Body*, (Boston, MA, Beacon Press, 1987); Aihwa Ong, *Spirits of Resistance and Capitalist Discipline*, (Albany, NY, SUNY Press, 1987); Shareon Traweek, *Beamtimes and Sometimes: The World of High-Energy Physicists*, (Cambridge, MA, Harvard University Press, 1988); Dorin Kondo, *Crafting Selves*, (Chicago, IL, The University of Chicago Press, 1990).

33. Hakken, 'Has there been a computer revolution?'; Pffafenberger, 'The social anthropology of technology'; Hess and Layne, *Knowledge and Society*; Hess, *Science and Technology in a Multicultural World*.

34. Haraway, *Symians, Cyborgs and Women*; Mary Jacobus, Evelyn Fox Keller and Sally Shuttleworth (eds), *Body/Politics. Women and the Discourses of Science*, (New York, Routledge, 1990); Keller, 'Nature, Nurture and the human genome project'.

35. These include Deborah Heath's study of a molecular biotechnology laboratory, (Deborah Heath, 'Computers' bodies: prosthesis and simultation in molecular biotechnology', presented at the panel 'Cyborg Anthropology II', 91st Annual Meeting of the American Anthropological Association, San Francisco, 1992); Barbara Joans' ethnography of virtual reality designers, (Barbara Joans, 'Outlaws and vigilantes in cyberspace', presented at the panel 'Virtual communities', 91st Annual Meeting of the American Anthropological Association, San Francisco, 2–6 December, 1992); and David West's research in progress on virtual reality users, (personal communication; for information on this project, contact David West at dmwest@stthomas.edu).

36. Sherry Turkle, *The Second Self. Computers and the Human Spirit*, (New York, Simon and Schuster, 1984).

37. Sherry Turkle, 'Living in the MUDs: multiplicity and identity in virtual reality', presented at the panel 'Cyborg Anthropology II', 91st Annual Meeting of the American Anthropological Association, San Francisco, 2–6 December 1992.

38. Brenda Laurel (ed.), *The Art of Human–Computer Interface Design*, (Reading, MA, Addison Wesley, 1990), p. 93.

39. Laurel, *The Art of Human–Computer Interface Design*, pp. 91–3.

40. Edward Barrett (ed.), *The Society of Text*, (Cambridge, MA, MIT Press, 1989) and John Walker, 'Through the looking glass', in Brenda Laurel (ed.), *The Art of Human–Computer Interface Design*, (Reading, MA, Addison Wesley, 1990), pp. 439–48.

41. John Barry, *Technobabble*, (Cambridge, MA, MIT Press, 1991).

42. Beatriz Sarlo, *La Imaginación Técnica. Sueños Modernos de la Cultura Argentina*, (Buenos Aires, Ediciones Nueva Visión, 1992).

43. Constance Penley and Andrew Ross (eds), *Technoculture*, (Minneapolis, MN, University of Minnesota Press, 1991); Henry Jenkins, *Textual Poachers*, (New York, Routledge, 1992).

44. John Fiske, Understanding Popular Culture, (Boston, MA, Unwin Hyman, 1989); Paul Willis, *Common Culture*, (Boulder, CO, Westview Press, 1990).

45. Mark Seltzer, *Bodies and Machines*, (New York, Routledge, 1992). Sarlo, *La Imaginación Técnica*; Jenkins, *Textual Poachers*.

46. John Gumperz, *Discourse Strategies*, (Berkeley, CA, University of California Press, 1983).

47. Alvarez, personal communication.

48. Barrett, *The Society of Text*; Alejandro Piscitelli, 'Los Hipermedios y el Placer del Texto Electrónico', *David y Goliath*, (Buenos Aires), No 58, pp. 64–78.

49. The linguistic anthropological investigation of cyberculture is clearly linked to the study of VCs, although not restricted to it. Alvarez claims that the characterisation of HCMC groups as 'virtual' communities is a misnomer, since from the perspective of linguistic interaction, HCMC groups are 'real' communities. A different question, about

the adequacy of the model of conversation for dealing with computers, has been posed by Walker, ('Through the looking glass', p. 443). 'When you are interacting with a computer', he says, 'you are not conversing with another person. You are exploring another world.' Here might lie some challenges for linguistic anthropology.

50. Pierre Lévy, 'La Oralidad Primaria, la Escritura y la Informática', *David y Goliath*, (Buenos Aires), No. 58, 1991, pp. 4–16.

51. Eric Wolf, *Europe and the People without History*, (New York and Berkeley, CA, University of California Press, 1982); William Roseberry, *Anthropologies and Histories: Essays in Culture, History, and Political Economy*, (New Brunswick, NJ, Rutgers University Press, 1992).

52. Mark Poster, *The Mode of Information. Poststructuralism and Social Context*, (Chicago, IL, The University of Chicago Press, 1990).

53. Gilles Deleuze, 'Control y Devenir. Entrevista con Toni Negri', translated by Edgar Garavito, *El Espectador. Magazin Dominical*, (Bogota), No 511, 7 February 1993, pp. 14–18.

54. David Ronfeldt, *Cyberocracy, Cyberspace, and Cyberology: Political Effects of the Information Revolution*, (Santa Monica, CA, The Rand Corporation, 1991).

55. Enrique Leff, *Ecología y Capital*, (Mexico, DF, UNAM, 1986); Godelier, '"Salt currency" and the circulation of commodities among the Baruya of New Guinea'.

56. Rabinow, 'Artificiality and enlightenment'.

57. Martin O'Connor, 'On the misadventures of capitalist nature', *Capitalism, Nature and Socialism*, 4(4), 1993, pp. 1–34; Escobar, 'From organism to cyborg'.

58. Vandana Shiva and Jack Kloppenburg, 'Alternative agriculture and the new biotechnologies', *Science as Culture*, 2(13), 1991, pp. 483–506.

59. Frederick Buttle, Martin Kenney and Jack Kloppenburg, 'From green revolution to biorevolution: some observations on the changing technological bases of economic transformation in the Third World', *Economic Development and Cultural Change*, 34, 1985, pp. 31–55.

60. Manuel Castells and Robert Laserna, 'The new dependency: technological change and socioeconomic restructuring in Latin America', *Sociological Forum*, 4(4), 1989, pp. 535–60.

61. Escobar, *Encountering Development*.

62. Judith Sutz, 'Los Cambios Tecnológicos y sus Impactos: Un Largo Camino Hacia la Construcción Solidaria de Oportunidades', *Fermentum*, (Caracas), 3(6/7), 1992, p. 138.

63. Ong, *Spirits of Resistance and Capitalist Discipline*; Maria Mies, *Patriarchy and Accumulation on a World Scale*, (London, Zed Books, 1986).

64. Lourdes Beneria and Shelly Feldman, *Unequal Burden*, (Boulder, CO, Westview Press, 1992).

65. Darnovsky *et al*, 'Radical Experiments. Social movements take on technoscience'.

66. Manuel de Landa, 'Nonorganic life', in Crary and Kwinter (eds), *Incorporations*, pp. 128–67.

67. M. Mitchell Waldrop, *Complexity. The Emerging Science at the Edge of Chaos*, (New York, Simon and Schuster, 1994). An introduction

to complexity for people with two or three years of college science is found in Grégoire Nicolis and Ilya Prigogine, *Exploring Complexity*, (New York, W H Freeman, 1989). See also Ziauddin Sardar and Jerome R Ravetz (eds), 'Complexity: fad or future', special issue, *Futures*, 26(6), July/August 1994.

68. Katherine Hayles, 'Introduction: complex dynamics in literature and science', in Katherine Hayles (ed.), *Chaos and Order. Complex Dynamics in Literature and Science*, (Chicago, IL, The University of Chicago Press, 1991), pp. 1–36; see also Stuart Kauffman, 'Antichaos and adaptation', *Scientific American*, 265(2), 1991, pp. 78–84.

69. Another attempt at relating complexity (particularly chaos) to the human sciences is Argyros's critique of deconstruction. Alexander Argyros, *A Blessed Rage for Order*, (Ann Arbor, MI, The University of Michigan Press, 1991).

70. Nicolis and Prigogine, *Exploring Complexity*, pp. 5–78.

71. Francisco Varela, 'The reenchantment of the concrete', in Crary and Kwinter (eds), *Incorporations*, pp. 320–39; Francisco Varela, Evan Thompson and Eleanor Rosch, *The Embodied Mind*, (Cambridge, MIT Press, 1991).

72. Foucault, *The Order of Things*.

73. Deleuze and Guattari, *A Thousand Plateaus*; Gilles Deleuze, *The Fold. Leibnitz and the Baroque*, (Minneapolis, MN, University of Minnesota Press, 1993).

74. Varela *et al*, *The Embodied Mind*.

75. See the volumes of the Santa Fe Institute Studies in the Sciences of Complexity. See, for instance, Philip Anderson, Kenneth Arrow and David Pines (eds), *The Economy as an Evolving Complex System*, (New York, Addison Wesley, 1983), for an application of complexity to economics. Work within the sciences themselves continues at a fast pace, including areas such as artificial life, adaptive computational models, autocatalysis, neural networks, cellular automata, emergence, coevolution, and the like.

76. Langdon Winner, 'If you liked chaos, you'll love complexity', *New York Times Book Review*, 14 February 1993, p. 12.

77. Ralph Trouillot, 'Anthropology and the savage slot: the poetics and politics of otherness', in Richard Fox (ed.), *Recapturing Anthropology*, (Santa Fe, NM, School of American Research, 1991).

78. Fox (ed.), *Recapturing Anthropology: Working in the Present*.

79. Science fiction, unfortunately, continues the traditional representation of others characteristic of nineteenth and twentieth century anthropology and fiction. In Gibson's work despite a multitude of new 'others', Jamaican 'zionites' and Haitian 'voodoites' retain exemplary status as exotic others.

CHAPTER 7

Is There a New Political Paradigm Lurking in Cyberspace?

Jay Kinney

It starts with a nagging feeling in your gut. You stand in the voting booth scanning the ballot, trying to recognise a familiar name or number. You can hear the people waiting impatiently in line outside and the sound reminds you of the lines for the bathroom at intermission during *Angels in America*. You just want to do your business and get out of there so that the next person in line can get in and have their moment of release. This is democracy? This is a pain in the neck. And all too often this is politics in America today.

So you hearken to the siren song of digital politics. Someone conjures up a vision of electronic democracy: Vote from the comfort of your own home! Take as long as you like to make your decisions! Access readily-available candidate information and statements online! E-mail your congressperson! Sign that electronic petition! Form *ad hoc* interest groups and virtual political parties! Debate the issues! Fax your grievances to Boris Yeltsin! Chat with Al Gore on AOL!

Yes, it's a thrilling scene with the socially-concerned family gathered around the ol' PC forging the politics of tomorrow. Why, I can feel the glow from here, but then that old nagging feeling starts up again and those haunting questions are back. Does this rosy scene have more than a snowball's chance in hell of actually happening? Whose vision is this anyway, and how much does all that hardware actually cost? What is going on?

Early on in one's confrontation with the marvellous digital future, one realises that this developing reality has at least two parallel tracks down which it's rushing simultaneously. Track A: the never ending wet dream of power, speed and wealth expanding exponentially for ever and ever. This is the world where we'll soon have Crays on our desktops; the World Wide Web will be the Ultimate Info Mall; Junior's savvy use of his *Grolier* CD-ROM will get him into Harvard; and for only a small fee you'll be able to do what you've always wanted – home banking! This is the vision of computer magazines, technology columnists, Pentium ads and user groups.

It's the adrenaline rush of more megabytes of RAM, more gigabytes of storage, and a ISDN line for Christmas. Chances are, if you are reading this, Track A is familiar turf. It's also the track of electronic politics: a grand empowered future is within our grasp! Let's call it airbrushed, backlit, future porn.

Track B is a bit less dazzling. It's the imploding nightmare of bankruptcy, frustration and fascism with the meter ticking and spiralling endlessly into the black hole at the centre of your wallet. This is the universe where your hard disk just munched itself without a backup; the latest version of Microsoft Word requires 26 megabytes of storage; you have to max out your credit card to get the PowerMac you need to keep up with the competition; and the NSA and FBI want to assure their access to everyone's private files 'just in case'. This is the reality of money laundering by electronic funds transfer, BBS busts by Tennessee prosecutors, Kevin Mitnick with your credit card number and press conferences by the Electronic Frontier Foundation. It's the grinding anxiety of viruses in your system, flame wars in your E-mailbox, and pinpoint bombing in this week's Third World country of choice. Again, chances are, you've got one foot in this world as well. Call it Digital Dystopia if you will.

Any serious look at how technology is shaping the American political landscape has to take both tracks into consideration. Track A for the promises being made and Track B for booby traps located in the fine print.

Although cultural critics announced some time ago the death of the avant-garde as an artistic force, the news has yet to penetrate the bastions of media where the concept of a 'cutting edge' still provides the rationale for marketing the ongoing cultural carnival of magazines, CDs, software and world views. During the heyday of modernism the old avant-garde served to critique the remnants of a cultural Academy steeped in bourgeois self-satisfaction. However the avant-garde was absorbed by the mass bohemian spasm of the counterculture at the close of the 1960s, and shortly thereafter the whole dream of a rebellious alternative culture mutated into mock-outrageous pop culture powered by the constant need for new things to sell. Somewhere in there, the avant-garde transmuted into the myth of the cutting edge.

During the 1970s, the mechanism for the evolution from avant-garde to cutting edge was facilitated by a treadmill of pop nostalgia which methodically gobbled up the previous decades of the twentieth century climaxing in a brief (and unnerving) embrace of the present during the Carter administration. This brief moment of real time was celebrated by the enforced donning of tractor or baseball caps by all Americans above the age of five. However, 1977 saw the emergence of two cultural icons that marked the coming shift from past and present to future tense: *Star Wars* and the Apple II. The allure of actually living in a sci-fi universe, now rendered both accessible and cuddly by George Lucas and Steve Jobs' mastery of the cute touch, was impossible to resist.

If literary science fiction in the hands of past masters like Frederick Pohl or Cordwainer Smith served as a social critique of the present in the guise of the future, pop sci-fi now became an invitation to trade in the past for a hopped up celebration of the still-to-come. Although intended as mockery, the media's characterisation of Reagan's proposed Strategic Defence Initiative as 'Star Wars' ended up cementing the marriage of convenience between sci-fi and future porn. By the time that Cyberpunk, *Bladerunner* and *Terminator* came along with their seductive cyborg nightmares the general population was primed for techno-lust. The cutting edge was rollerblading down both Tracks A and B and there would be no looking back. The identification of digital culture as the wave of the future was complete.

Cupertino is not Akron. As the old messy technology of heavy industry was dying in the ageing Rust Belt back East and shifting to cheaper venues abroad, it was somehow fitting that the culture of infinite possibilities would spring up in the Far West. Silicon Valley in the 1980s was a heady place, an amazing electromagnet for venture capital. With all that capital pouring in, the contagious belief that anything could happen (and indeed sometimes did) spread like wildfire. Early video game programmers made their fortunes in royalties, home computing hot shots built up companies out of thin air, and Steve Wozniak had sufficient funds to bankroll the Us Festival, a nerd's version of Woodstock. Horatio Alger was reborn in an alligator shirt and whatever the state of the steel mills in Pittsburgh, things looked sweet on the Peninsula.

Dreams die hard, and although some of yesterday's brightest high tech stars have subsequently plummeted to earth and the era of overnight success in software and gadgetry is long since gone, the fact remains that computers and consumer electronics are one of the few places in the economy where products continue to improve while prices drop. It's as if, at least in this niche, the ideals of competition, creativity and progress still seem to magically work.

Small wonder then, that Silicon Valley continues to be a fount of inspiration and validation for America's beloved myth of work and success. The corporate culture that has inevitably settled in is still looser than in most older industries and the breakneck pace of change provides a heady sense of momentum unimpeded by stick-in-the-mud factors like trade unions. Since many of the key players in the field do not fit the cliché of drab businessmen and the technology keeps topping itself in smart-aleck fashion, the glowing self-image generated on Track A almost necessitates the idea that there is a new improved politics emerging in the midst of gung-ho digital culture. This notion is even more seductive if one zeroes in on digital culture's cutting edge: cyberspace. However, the closer one looks, the more dicey the proposition becomes.

About the time that CNN viewers got to witness ecstatic Germans capering around on top of the Berlin Wall, it became clear that politics as usual was haemorrhaging severely. The poor performance of the Socialists in power in France and Italy, and the collapse of Soviet Communism and its satellites delivered a swift kick to the nuts of leftists everywhere. The sheer exuberance of the citizens of the Eastern Bloc as they busted free from their ideological chains was contagious and it nearly did in the Left as a credible player in the political arena. Even Sweden, everyone's favourite welfare state, underwent a mini-revolution and voted the long-reigning Social Democrats out of power.

Ironically, the apparent demise of Communism as a galvanising enemy rendered a delayed body blow to the Right as well. Conservatives began to fight among themselves over the next step to take, opening up a rift between neocons and paleocons. Free market visionaries and investors who had been talking a good game in Gorbachev's final days, ploughed head first into the dung heap of Russia's chaotic economy under Yeltsin. And George Bush, who announced the arrival of the New World Order, was unable to sustain the afterglow from Reagan's revolution for more than one term.

Fast forward to the present stand-off with a Democratic president, a Republican Congress, and more voters than ever registering as 'Independent'. Momentary crowing among the Republicans over the 1994 elections aside, one gets the sense that given half a chance the electorate would love to ditch the old Left/Right horseshoe match and try on some new paradigms altogether.

In 1992, Ross Perot spoke to this craving, emulating a kind of pure American pragmatism beyond ideology. However the plucky little billionaire made an awkward populist and had too much other baggage, most notably a bad haircut and a bad temper, to serve as anything other than a spoiler. Still, the frustration with politics as usual lives on, translated into a generalised 'anti-government mood' as it's been dubbed by the media. Which, one would think, would result in scores of voters embracing the Libertarian Party, the most explicitly anti-government electoral vehicle around, and the main political entity claiming to be neither left nor right.

Think again. Although there's currently an upsurge of pundit-chat about the possible rise of a major third party in the next election, both hostile state electoral rules and pervasive media scepticism are stacked against it. Besides, a third party President,

unaccompanied by a supporting wave of successful third party
congressmen and senators, would be even more thwarted than
Clinton. Minus a breakthrough in grassroots organising, the
Libertarian Party – like other third parties – limps along, its most
palatable rhetoric co-opted by politicians outside its ranks. By
default the disgruntled crowd ends up voting against whoever is
in power or not voting at all. And so the game staggers on zombie-
like, sapped of real will or credibility.

Less is More

Which leads some visionaries to theorise that maybe the high tech
juggernaut – especially the online parts – will break the stasis and
usher the world into a crackerjack new era of digital democracy.
After all, you don't have to be inordinately rich in order to open a
Web site, or a BBS, or to spout off in online forums. Maybe this
is the grand opportunity for new political paradigms and ideologies
to coalesce and to strut their stuff before an appreciative citizenry.
As you'll recall, one of Perot's most memorable flourishes was a
call for Electronic Democracy.

Colorado bulletin board maven Dave Hughes helped get a 'Perot
for President' BBS set up during the 1992 campaign and is second
to none in touting the potential virtues of a wired populace. For
Hughes, 'Electronic Democracy simply means using … two-way
electronic means to permit the voting public to participate actively
and not passively in the public debate, discussions … and analysis
of issues, candidates, and public matters.' It is, 'above all, a renewal
of the idea that individuals count again in the political process, and
have the power to participate, through electronic devices they have
access to.'[1]

Certainly the political voices that can be encountered in
cyberspace seem diverse, although recent polls are of little help in
determining concrete numbers. A mid-1994 survey of Internet
users by three academic researchers found that their political party
affiliations roughly matched those of the general population: 36
per cent Democrat, 32 per cent Independent and 23 per cent
Republican.[2] When *Wired* magazine recently conducted an informal
E-mail poll among a cross-section of participants in the budding
digital culture, no clear-cut political identity emerged. 'Liberal',
'progressive', 'libertarian', 'anarchist' and 'conservative', all scored
between 10 per cent and 17 per cent as self-applied labels, while
a sizeable chunk came up with intriguing if indecipherable
oxymorons: 'Progressive conservative'; 'Virtual Populist'; 'market-
oriented progressive'; and the ever popular 'Anarcho-emergentist
Republican'.[3] The most common perception of the brand of politics

dominating the Net is one of radical libertarianism or a mix of extreme liberals and extreme conservatives with very little in the middle. People most attracted to the Internet are largely from the fringes of society – folks who, for one reason or another, feel their message is not represented by the mainstream media. They have been described as 'bandwidth hogs' as they tend to use the Net like a megaphone to broadcast their extreme views. This is not altogether surprising: if a new inchoate politics is percolating among people who, whether justifiably or not, feel disturbed by the drift of the culture, this politics is likely to erupt in non-mainstream and off-centre ways, otherwise it wouldn't be new. This may not exactly be what the advocates of electronic democracy have in mind, but it does correlate with the popularity of, say, Rush Limbaugh: a lot of mid-Americans are royally pissed off and the emerging digital culture is one arena for that discontent.

Cyberspace is often characterised by observers as a new frontier with the 'Don't Tread On Me' vigour of the Green Mountain Boys and the old Wild West. While international in scope, the Net has been dominated so far by American voices and sites. Perhaps its new politics is not so new at all, but rather the resurfacing of a doughty American anarchism – a pioneer/settler philosophy of self-reliance, direct action and small-scale decentralism translated into pixels. After all, the relatively wide open nature of it during its early years meant you could stake your claim in some obscure corner of the Net and be the ruler of your own virtual realm.

Science writer, Simson L. Garfinkel observes: 'Information Technology seems to have attracted strong, aggressive, male, radical Libertarian types. I suspect that this is because it is attracting people who feel comfortable dominating: they dominate technology, they dominate those around them, they feel comfortable taking charge and control of things. I also believe that Information Technology makes people this way. This is because ... it gives you the power to work your will on your environment. You can shut people up by pressing the 'D' key or putting their name in your kill file.'[4]

Although originally funded by government sources, the Internet's decentralised, cooperative structure has been, ironically, the closest thing to a functioning large-scale anarchist society that human culture has yet seen. While the offline society-at-large seems bogged down in a bewildering swamp of regulation, litigation, legislative gridlock and intrusive social engineering, the relatively blank canvas of the Net has encouraged visionaries to project their dreams of a new political order.

These dreams take several forms. Track A visionaries such as Marilyn Davis, author of the eVote software for online voting, are certain that the political process, including elections themselves, will be enhanced by the expansion of cyberspace. Davis explains: 'In the not-too-distant future, the people in the online communities will band together to get their candidates elected to every office in every (somewhat) democratic country. These new "politicians" will be the puppets of the online democratic community and they will, as much as possible, hand over all their power to the online community. People who are not online will vote for our candidates because they hate politicians. And because Our system will be wonderfully benevolent.'[5]

Davis, bless her heart, is quite sincere. So is Jim Warren, founder of Infoworld and the Computers, Freedom & Privacy conferences, although he doesn't go quite so far in his goals. Having masterminded online pressure that led to the California Legislature making information on bills, amendments, votes, etc. available on the Net, Warren is orchestrating support for the expansion of information available through the US Congress's Thomas World Wide Web page. Warren's goal includes making available online transcripts of House and Senate C-Span programs, the Congressional Record, extensive information about all registered lobbyists, and much more. With all this information at our fingertips, Warren hopes that 'we may be able to see it in time to effectively participate in the process of our own governance through irresistible grassroots action.'[6]

But such optimism calls for a dose of Track B pessimism to keep things in perspective. Given that probably only 5 per cent of the population even owns a modem, if that, these envisioned grassroots remain pretty rarefied. Yet even this minute upsurge of activity may backfire. Simson L. Garfinkel cautions: 'I know that most Congressional staffers simply dread the day that constituents are able to send E-mail to senators and congressmen. I was speaking to one staffer the other day, who said that they were simply deluged with letters and telephone calls now; they can't give out the fax number for fear that the fax will become unusable. She is terrified that the level of mail will increase by a factor of two or three once they go online ... She said that they might have to stop their policy of returning a personalised letter to every letter that they get.' Garfinkel continues: 'I believe that easier access to our representatives will have the result of lowering their accountability and interest in voter feedback. It will do this by lowering the communications barrier between the representatives and the people, thus raising the noise level. We have seen the same thing happening on the Internet.'[7] Virtual reality researcher Robert Jacobson is even more pessimistic about political things to come: 'The grassroots opinions are going to become increasingly irrelevant, except at regular booster sessions called to stand in for vital political debate.

Elections will be for functionaries to argue the cases of their respective corporate patrons.'8

In any event, whether you are seized with electronic optimism or pessimism, it is best to remember that the politics that we bring to cyberspace is only half the picture. The politics that the burgeoning technology is enacting upon us as it spreads its tendrils everywhere looms larger still. Let's cut away for a bit from the microcosmic vision of votes, civic debates and mid-America with modems, and consider the bigger picture, for there is compelling evidence of global forces at work which dwarf the self-conceptions or ideological intentions of any one group of individuals. This is the politics of historical currents, not Net-surfing soapboxes.

Think Locally, Act Globally

Futurists make much of the collapse of time and space that is being ushered in by world telecommunications and the microchip. As anyone who has stuck their finger in the socket of the Internet can testify, the heady sense of personal power that results from zipping back and forth from FTP sites in Europe to Web pages in Vancouver is dazzling – at least initially. However the power of virtual mobility is not quite the same as the power of accumulated capital. At the same time that you may be downloading an enormous video clip of Tonya Harding's wedding night courtesy of some Net server five states away, multinational corporations are busily conducting transactions worth millions of dollars in the blink of an eye.

Cyberspace is full of armchair mavericks and eccentric ideologues. But whatever the gyrations of political difference and originality among them, the onrushing logic of the integration of the world economy and world politics into a single unified whole may overshadow those distinctions, just as the boundaries between nations are becoming anachronistic in the face of the 'global marketplace'.

It's at this point in the discussion that things begin to get a little hairy. Political minds of a certain 'patriotic' turn, be they Birchers in the US or Pamyat in Russia, catch a whiff of this creeping globalisation in the wake of the Cold War's demise and the ascendancy of international networking, and start shouting about nefarious conspiracies to do in their respective motherlands. Since talk of international conspiracies smacks of paranoia, scapegoating, or worse, these naysayers to the New World Order are immediately dismissed as reactionary nutcases.

However, this may be a case of tossing the baby out with the bathwater. True, the illuminati may not exist and the thought of some hidden directorate craftily coordinating everything from the

Savings & Loan debacle to the spread of Aids is a mite hard to swallow. Yet, like the Internet itself, the process of global integration may have no directing centre on which to pin the blame, but merely its own internal logic and the confluence of self-interested economic and political entities. This may be quite sufficient to overturn the old order.

When queried about the future of nationalism, Lawrence Wilkinson, co-founder of the Net-wise Global Business Network, encapsulates it thus:

> Just as during the Enlightenment 'the nation-state' took over from 'the church' to become the dominant seat of action, so the nation-state is now receding, yielding center stage to 'the marketplace'; the action in the marketplace is interestingly everywhere: local, global, wherever – where 'wherever' is increasingly dictated by 'pure' economics and interests, not by national borders ... I believe that we're in for some nationalist noise and some nationalist violence before the transition is done, but I do believe that it will finish, to be replaced by the kinds of tribal and commercial conflicts described by folks like Joel Kotkin (author of *Tribes*) and Charles Hampden-Turner and Fons Trompenaur (authors of *Seven Cultures of Capitalism*). What will remain of nationalism? My bet is that it'll have the character – the strength and relative 'weight' – of brand loyalty; perhaps in some cases, that charged variety of brand loyalty, a fan's relationship to a sports team.[9]

It's funny that Wilkinson should mention sports and brand loyalty because that very area may provide an incongruous example of what's under way. As it turns out, shoe companies and sportswear makers are spending millions of dollars to assure that football, basketball and other teams wear their brands of logo-emblazoned apparel on the field as a form of quasi-subliminal advertising. As John Flinn recently reported in the *San Francisco Examiner*, 'Shoe companies actually file "starting lineups" before each game with NFL Properties. Nike and Reebok are allowed to have ten players on each team displaying their logos. Players not under contract are allowed to wear Adidas or other brands on the field, but only if the logos are covered with tape.'[10]

In other words, as nationalism becomes mere brand loyalty, brand loyalty becomes the new nationalism. Inner city gangs are already hip to this development. Just ask the school kid who's been shot for wearing the wrong sports jacket. This is also the peculiar truth that reactionaries intuit when they conjure up visions of the Universal Price Code as the Mark of the Beast. Nature abhors a vacuum and as the old icons of flag and family blink out there are plenty of registered trademarks to take their place.

Perhaps I exaggerate, but still, with the old nationalist boundaries dissolving – on the Web, in the market, on TV – suddenly you are face to face with the only boundary left that counts: the boundary between your mind and the rest of the world. Prepare for psychic colonisation wherein every moment bears the stamp of some corporate sponsor or other. The A&E or Fox Network 'bugs' in the corner of your TV screen (or the ad strips across the top of *HotWired* World Wide Web screens for that matter) are only the beginning.

Okay. Let's see if we can take this planetary Track B nightmare and boil it down into a single equation: Digital Revolution = Global Integration = New World Order = Marketplace Über Alles. Shades of *Neuromancer*.

Is this a credible bogeyman? While sceptics may reserve judgement, we can already detect signs of convergence of interest implied here. Arthur Kroker, who is admittedly about as close to sci-fi as you can get in the academic world of postmodern theory, offers a couple of specific examples of transnational integration. Kroker points to the growth of a 'new global technological élite' (which he calls the 'virtual class') who see the Net as an opportunity to 'maximise pure business interests. [Their] motto is: "Adapt or You're Toast." For example, British Air[ways] uses the information superhighway to relocate its worldwide reservation service to India in order to take advantage of cheap labour and, in the near future, Africa will be used as a base for surveillance systems for US malls, thus hard-wiring cheap labour to the information superhighway.'[11] What is this if not simultaneous decentralisation and integration? In similar fashion, a junior executive who telecommutes from home is less beholden to the geographical location of corporate headquarters, but he is all the more dependent on the network of technology and information that underpins the process.

According to David Ronfeldt, the growth of cyberspace and the information-based society generate 'forces (that) disrupt and erode hierarchies, diffuse and redistribute power, redraw boundaries, broaden spatial and temporal horizons, and compel closed systems to open up. This creates troubles especially for large, bureaucratic, aging institutions...' From a positive perspective, Ronfeldt suggests that such troubles 'favor the rise of multi-organizational networks of small organizations' which are able to act together at a distance through networked links.[12] Score one for the little guy.

However, in terms of possible negative outcomes he also cites and paraphrases Daniel Bell's 1977 warnings about destabilisation. This has more immediate domestic implications and brings us back to the question of emerging politics. Ronfeldt writes: 'Societies, the United States in particular, are undergoing a "loss of insulating space" as conditions and events in one place are quickly, demandingly communicated to other places. Political systems are becoming more "permeable" than ever to destabilising events, and people are more able to respond directly and immediately. In some societies – Bell was worried about the United States – this may raise the likelihood of contagious mass reactions and mobilisations, and make the rulers strengthen centralised controls to keep that from occurring.'[13]

With all the encouragement coming from Al Gore, Newt Gingrich and Co. for the Infobahn to come, it would seem as if contagious mobilisations and destabilisations are the last thing that the Government is worried about. Not so. The NSA and FBI had at least one eye on such possibilities, along with more garden variety crimes and mischief when they proposed the clipper chip and Digital Telephony Act. And more efforts at control, both cultural and political, are coming fast and furious. To those in charge, any change in the distribution of power or secrecy is destabilising.

But don't PGP encryption and the decentralised nature of the Internet assure freedom of speech and ward off attempts at control? Not really. A radar detector can help warn you of speed traps but the highway patrol will still arrest and prosecute you if they discover you have one in your car. PGP may enable you to exchange mail securely with a friend but it doesn't help much if what you exchange is defined as illegal and your hard disk is seized.

The shorthand term 'Infobahn' summons up visions of the German Autobahn – an atypical stretch of road with no speed limits. But much of US highway still has 55 mph speed limits. Everyone ignores those limits but only at the sufferance of the cops. As the info superhighway comes into view our lawmakers are hustling to jump on their motorbikes and start issuing tickets. Thus, legislative efforts are already under way to make it a felony to transmit files, E-mail or images deemed unacceptable. A few pivotal lawsuits and court cases may throw the fear of God into the rising telecomglomerates real quickly, rendering unpopular speech on the Net an activity dangerous to one's health. If a local Tennessee prosecutor (with the assistance of the Justice Department) can successfully convict a California adult BBS for obscenity, how much longer before the clean-up crews start going after the alt.binaries newsgroups on the Net?

And that's just the attacks from above. Online warfare from private parties is also gearing up. Recently someone apparently sympathetic to the Church of Scientology unleashed a cancelbot on the Internet to delete all Usenet postings they considered injurious to the Church's name and property. The Church even went so far as to persuade Finnish police to wrest the identity of an anonymous poster to alt.scientology from the confidential files of anon.penet.fi, the anonymous E-mail remailer in Finland. And greencard lawyer Martha S. Siegel, of Canter and Siegel spamming notoriety, demanded in an op-ed piece in newspapers across the country that Internet be put under FCC control and that the same anonymous server in Finland be demolished through diplomatic pressure.[14] In other words, the Net's days as a free zone may be rapidly drawing to a close, and instead of electronic democracy we may find ourselves catapulted into a surreal mix of psychowar and corporate feudalism.

Before you kindly wipe the foam from my mouth, consider this: as any social studies teacher can tell you (and probably did at some point) the foundations of traditional democracy derive from electing representatives who presume to speak for discrete real-world communities and are pledged to defend their interests – or at least help them mesh with those of the greater good. Thus the shift towards a world of atomised individuals linked primarily in *ad hoc* and transitory virtual communities is a step away from the context in which democracy makes most sense.

No matter how much legislative information is available online, it is basically superfluous if you don't have the time or desire to access it, digest it and weigh your options. Unfortunately the network-induced collapse of time doesn't deliver more time – it takes it away by speeding everything up. This quickening is grand for those who are poised to leap on each new innovation and exploit it profitably, but it doesn't help much in building a new politics which goes beyond blowing off steam in alt.conspiracy.

As for political watchdogging? Former CIA analyst Robert D. Steele has proposed an 'Open Source Intelligence' strategy which helps trim intelligence agency budgets and excessive covert bravura by redirecting intelligence gathering towards the Net.[15] One OSI proposal by Steele's associate Anthony Fedanzo suggests

> the constituents of the proposed OSI organization will be electronically linked, geographically dispersed, predominantly unpaid amateurs from the standpoint of present intelligence professionals. OSI participants will be citizen analysts, a term describing persons whose primary activity in life is not the collection, analysis, and presentation of intelligence, but some other way of life and employment. Citizen analysts will be free of employment contracts, performance reviews (except *de facto* reviews by their peers and information requesters), and all statutory obligations beyond those already existing for civilised behaviour. They are at liberty to work with whatsoever information tools, techniques, methods, and resources they select. Citizen analysts are required to use OSI standard exchange formats and media for OSI products.

On the other side of the ledger, citizen analysts will not be able to charge expenses. Nor may they claim any form of compensation now or in the future from the OSI organisation. They will receive a fixed minimum number of free hours of connect time to the OSI network.

Ideally, the incentive for participants consists of social recognition and psychological rewards stemming from voluntary service to the nation. More pragmatically, requesters could contract directly with citizen analysts or consortia of analysts for follow-on studies. Commercial firms that allow employees a few hours a week to participate might receive R&D tax credits, or the like. The OSI organisation will need to receive a small percentage (say, 1–2 per cent) of any fees paid to OSI participants when those fees result from work gained through participation in the OSI network.[16]

In other words, amateur spies – excuse me, citizen analysts – may keep tabs on the far-flung Net in return for free connect time and that sense of patriotic pride. It's enough to give a new meaning to the phrase, 'inquiring minds want to know!'

Make no mistake, the Internet is not the end-all and be-all of digital culture, it is just the current boxing ring where the rationalisation of cyberspace is being hammered out. One is reminded of Mao's strategic campaign to 'let a thousand flowers bloom', which flushed out all the troublemakers who then had nowhere to hide when the worm turned.

Perhaps reflecting the polarised mix of ideological proponents who populate the Net, the *de facto* politics of cyberspace has until now been an amalgam of anal retentive libertarianism and liberal altruism. You could more or less do what you liked online, as long as you played by the rules, channelled your anti-social and deviant impulses into obscure alt.hierarchy newsgroups, and didn't get the wrong sysops mad at you. It's all been rather like an enormous floating sci-fi convention by modem, which is just about what you'd expect from a milieu that was originally devised by people whose idea of fun was reading *Dune* at two in the morning while waiting for their code to compile.

Yet, when you get down to brass tacks, it seems as if such *laissez-faire* pluralism is not so much the wave of the future as an artefact of an odd fleeting interlude in the late twentieth century when Queen Unix ruled the Net and the Chancellor of the Exchequer was off at a Mensa meeting. Perhaps in the same way that artists and bohemians serve as unwitting advance scouts for urban neighbourhood gentrification, the cutting edge technopagans and netheads are actually homing devices for the waves of MBAs and lawyers coming to settle cyberspace. If they're lucky, the original natives of the Net – the grad students and the hackers who devised freeware like Archie and invented the Usenet binaries groups – will be allowed to retire to a reservation in some obscure corner of the Global Village, there to grep and ping like their ancestors before them. Everyone else will be busy shopping online, playing 'Doom', and keeping tabs on each other.

'My My My', said the Spider to the Fly

Then again, the very term 'online' may rapidly become obsolete if current trends continue. Consider the following projections and spin your own scenario. If we assume that: both co-axial cable and wireless grids spread to quasi-Universal access (already in motion); bandwidth widens to allow the equivalent of HDTV on your desktop (only a matter of time); your desktop decentralises and mobilises through miniaturisation, voice recognition and 'smart' interfaces to usher in television with schedule-based programming and distinct commercials at measured intervals, and mutates into a selection of interactive 24-hour lifestyle choices sponsored by vast competing corporate alliances who help you to literally 'get a life' (foreshadowed in TCI-Sprint or Microsoft Net ventures coming into view); electronic money, smart cards, and various tax agencies collaborate to marginalise cash while assuring that the City/State/Federal/and (in due course) World tax authorities get their cut of every financial or commodity transaction (still working the bugs out of this one); and that one way or the other, nothing is free – that is, the meter is running on all services rendered all the time, although we may toggle between productive 'billable' time (when we build up our credit reservoir) and leisure 'consumption' time (when our reservoir is drawn upon); and when IRC, phone sex, CB radio, TV talk shows, and talk radio all coalesce into an array of 24-hour pick-a-peer channels you can patch into anywhere with your wireless headset, and the dividing line between virtual reality and real life becomes mostly academic; and when the whole hassle over sampling, copying, digitising, intellectual property rights and licensing gets ironed out in some grand ASCAP-like registry scheme where consumers subscribe to licensing banks which grant them usage rights over all media with that bank's logo-stamp (Bill Gates is already heading in this direction). Well, then, where does that leave us?

In such a future – an instrumentalised, administered, metered, and market-defined future to be sure, when Track A and Track B are so inextricably interwoven that leaving the Net becomes as unthinkable as giving up breathing – where is the place for politics, new or otherwise?

The whole thrust of the major player, video-on-demand, totally wired, multimedia, content-provider blitzkrieg is an entertainment-saturated environment that leaves little time or space for debate and studied thought about 'issues'. The increasingly complex decisions required by a global civilisation will likely be left to the policy wonks, CEOs and the institutional minions who keep the whole ball rolling anyway. Choices like 'more' or 'less' government become obsolete when the technocratic, quasi-parental, service-marked colossus reduces your decision-making capacity to the level of 'would you like milk or sugar with your Prozac?' As the warp and the woof draw ever tighter, the feelings of claustrophobia and manipulation that result may indeed trigger a new politics in the midst of digital culture: the networked equivalent of the Branch Davidians, where the ultimate political gesture is one of withdrawal and self-marginalisation. But even self-exile to a private MUD counts for little when the Feds come knocking, as the ghost of David Koresh reminds us.

Meanwhile, netsurfing is an undeniable kick. All that psychic space to move around in is seductive in the extreme and at least in plugged-in urban areas it's actually cheaper to maintain a SLIP or PPP connection than it is to watch cable TV. But that too may change.

After all, repeat customers are the model citizens of the global market-place and addiction is the unspoken motif of the cuddly control that has got us in its grip. Libertarians love to point out that 'there ain't no such thing as a free lunch', though that's not always true. With drug dealers 'the first one's free', and it's a humdinger. The price goes up on the second visit. Perhaps the World Wide Web will be like really good crack: cheap and affordable until you're thoroughly addicted, then you wake up one day to discover the meter ticking and you've got an insatiable hunger for online infomercials.

One doesn't want to take this addiction metaphor too far – rampant accusations of addiction being the moral vice of the late twentieth century – but there is more than a passing resemblance to the junkie's build-up of drug tolerance and raised buzz threshold in the accelerating pace of innovation and throughput which drives digital culture forward. 'You gotta let me have more RAM, Frank! I can't get off on only eight megs anymore!'

And this is ultimately how the political lid is kept screwed on, no matter what label you choose. If your food and rent are dependent on E-mail and electronic currency and if your contact with friends and family is largely via cyberspace, then it's a good bet that you'll be dependably sitting at your PC most of the day, beholden to a global system which fits you like a snug logoed shoe. In such a universe the only political opposition not vulnerable to having its electricity shut off may be quirky Third World despots like Gaddafi who stand and heckle the advancing New World Order from the side of the road. And that is not a comforting thought.

But perhaps this is all too pessimistic, too Track B. Perhaps object-oriented programming and parallel processing will trickle down to where we can all create the decor of our own virtual universes and your E-mail gripe to your congressman will indeed make it through the maze and fulfil the promise of electronic democracy. Unfortunately, I have a recurring dream where the new political paradigm is already in place: you have to wear Nikes and I have to wear Reeboks – it's in the fine print of our software licences. As for the technopeasants who are stuck swapping old 2400 baud modems down at the fleamarket in the vacant lot? They have to tape up their logos when the camera's on them and just say 'cheese'.

Anyone care for an hors-d'oeuvre?

Notes

1. Dave Hughes posting in Politics conference, topic 25: 'Designing an Electronic Democracy: What Does It Really Mean?' on The Well, 14 June 1992.
2. Bonnie Fisher, Michael Margolis and David Resnick, 'A new way of talking politics: Democracy on the Internet', a paper delivered at the Annual Meeting of the American Political Science Association, 1–4 September 1994.
3. Private poll conducted by Jay Kinney and Kevin Kelly, November 1994.
4. *Ibid.*
5. *Ibid.*
6. *Ibid.*
7. *Ibid.*
8. *Ibid.*
9. *Ibid.*
10. John Flinn, 'The Logo Bowl', *San Francisco Examiner*, 15 January 1995, p. D–1.
11. Private interview with the author, November 1995.
12. David Ronfeldt, 'Cyberocracy is Coming', *Information Society Journal*, vol. 8, no. 4, pp. 243–96.
13. *Ibid.*
14. Martha S. Siegel, 'Anarchy, Chaos on the Internet Must End', *San Francisco Chronicle*, 2 January 1995.
15. Robert D. Steele, 'E3I: Ethics, Ecology, Evolution, and Intelligence', *Whole Earth Review*, Fall 1992, pp. 74–9.
16. Anthony Fedanzo, 'Implementing Open Source Intelligence Through a Distributed Contribution Model', available on The Well's gopher site, 1994.

Notes on Contributors

Nigel Clark is in the Department of Sociology at the University of Auckland, New Zealand. He has written on the interaction of environmental visions and computer-assisted realities.

Arturo Escobar teaches anthropology at the University of Massachusetts; he has studied 'modernisation' as a total cultural, political and technical phenomenon.

Jay Kinney is Publisher/Editor in Chief of *GNOSIS: A Journal of Western Inner Traditions*, in San Francisco.

Jerome R. Ravetz is the author of *Scientific Knowledge and its Social Problems* (Oxford University Press, 1971; Transaction Publishers 1996), and (with S.O. Funtowicz) *Uncertainty and Quality in Science for Policy*.

Ziauddin Sardar has written extensively on Information Technology, Third World Issues, Islam, and their connections. He is the joint author of *Barbaric Others* (Pluto Press, 1993)

Vivian Sobchack is a Professor in the School of Theater, Film, and Television, University of California at Los Angeles; her most recent book is *The Address of the Eye: a Phenomenology of Film Experience* (Princeton University Press, 1992).

George Spencer lives and works in Leeds, England; he has experience of the practice, teaching and theoretical analysis of Information Technology.

Index

Index by Judith Lavender